More advance praise for *Breathe*

"Dr. Vranich has managed to lay out a convincing, accessible, and friendly guide to making friends with your breath. This is the book to give to someone who suffers from stress, headaches, sleeplessness, or any of the multitude of modern-day ills, yet hasn't made the connection between these conditions and something very simple: poor breathing patterns. Every single cell in the human body requires oxygen to create energy—learning to breathe more effectively may be the best thing you ever do for improving your health."

—Donna Farhi, author of *The Breathing Book*

"*Breathe* expertly combines relevant science, repeated inspiration, and pinpoint guidance to propel readers to develop a fundamental tool to restore their health: a regular breathing practice. With this book, Dr. Belisa Vranich lays out in plain English—and wonderful humor—how to reclaim your vitality and reboot your body by doing something we all forgot how to do long ago—breathe!"

—Anthony J. Lyon, M.D.,
Medical Director, The Ash Center, NYC

"I was smiling—and breathing!—as I read Dr. Belisa's wonderful book, *Breathe*. With a great sense of humor, and an even greater understanding of her craft, she reminds us how breathing is our birthright, despite its neglect by modern (wo)man. She further connects us to our breath with relevant *hows* and *whys,* and empowers us to reclaim respiration with practical exercises. A full, deep breath benefits us on so many levels; I frequently recommend breathwork to patients and am delighted to now be able to recommend this book."

—Stephanie Marango, M.D., RYT,
founder of i.m.body and author of *Your Body and The Stars*

"Over the last few years, it's been refreshing to see some individuals in the fitness industry shedding light on the importance of proper breathing and the benefits it has on one's overall well-being. *Breathe* differentiates itself from the pack in its thorough explanation of proper body mechanics. I've had the fortunate experience of working and studying with Dr. Belisa, and as a result have had tremendous success with my own training as a martial artist, fitness enthusiast, and firefighter. I have also applied her methods in training clients, students, and probationary firefighters in understanding the proper breathing techniques, which has led to their own success. *Breathe* will teach the beginner and the elite athlete alike how to take the necessary steps in an easy-to-understand system to feeling and looking better."   —Joe March, Firefighter,
NASM, CPT, CES, MMASC, BJJ black belt

"Dr. Belisa Vranich draws on her years of clinical knowledge, skills, and insights to provide critical information in a direct way. *Breathe* equips us with essential and innovative tools that allow us to rejuvenate our physical and mental well-being."
—Dr. Adeyinka M. Akinsulure-Smith, senior supervising
psychologist at the Bellevue/NYU Program for Survivors of
Torture and associate professor at the City College of New York
and The Graduate Center, City University of New York

"The concept of breathing awareness may strike some readers as far-fetched and unsubstantiated by scholarly research, but Vranich will win them over with her detailed descriptions of strenuous-sounding but practical exercises to expand lung capacity and improve diaphragm strength. For those suffering from shortness of breath or ailments related to breathing or core strength, this work and its accompanying exercises depict an appealing and methodical program for improvement."   —*Publishers Weekly*

"With her remarkable talent for making important health information poignant and practical, Dr. Belisa is a wealth of information like no other." —Lisa Oz, radio and television personality, six-time *New York Times* bestselling author of several books including the You: The Owner's Manual series

"Innovative and effective stress relief. Amazing experience. It made such a difference in my clarity and energy. Just spectacular!" —Dr. Mathew Reid, Capt., U.S. Army Medical Corps, Emergency Department, Atlanta, Georgia

"I left Dr. Belisa's feeling like I was walking on air." —Drew Grant, staff writer for the *New York Observer*

"A light-headed, blissed-out state that, for some, borders on hallucinogenic. Even Xanax can't compare." —Katie Becker, *W* magazine

"Successful, long-term weight loss needs you to address your stress/cortisol levels as cortisol causes your body to hold on to fat. Breathwork and meditation is the most successful way to do this, and Dr. Belisa teaches this in an easy, fast way. Many of my clients have worked directly with Dr. Belisa and see immediate results in not just their waistline, but in their overall happiness! Bravo, Belisa, for showing us how!" —Lyn-Genet, author of *New York Times* bestseller *The Plan: Eliminate the Surprising "Healthy" Foods That Are Making You Fat—and Lose Weight Fast*

"Dr. Belisa is an incredibly open and gifted healer of others and her book is full of her amazing wisdom!" —David Elliot, healer and author of *Reluctant Healer* and *Healing*

"We are living at a time when we are so caught up in 'doing things' and trying to keep up with the rapid escalation of information and media that we often forget to stay connected to that which is most essential—*breathing*. Rudolph Steiner informs us that the average person breathes 25,900 times daily. How we breathe has a radical influence on the balance of our autonomic nervous system, our acid/alkaline balance, our digestion and elimination, and our posture and the muscles themselves. Dr. Belisa Vranich has put together a simple, effective program to help anyone learn to breathe effectively, which is an essential first step to body-mind integration."

—Paul Chek, Holistic Health Practitioner and founder of the C.H.E.K Institute

"This was the most effective class I've ever taken. It changed the way I felt instantaneously."   —Julia Edelstein, *Real Simple*, staff health editor

"Dr. Belisa's class helped alleviate my sciatica like no other treatment, so I was able to perform at Carnegie Hall once again! It is extraordinary."   —Ieva Siuksta, violinist, The Manhattan Symphony Orchestra, New York City

BREATHE

The Simple, Revolutionary
14-Day Programme to Improve Your
Mental and Physical Health

Belisa Vranich PsyD

HAY HOUSE

Carlsbad, California • New York City • London
Sydney • Johannesburg • Vancouver • New Delhi

First published and distributed in the United States of America by:
St. Martin's Press, 175 Fifth Avenue, New York, N.Y. 10010;
www.stmartins.com

First published and distributed in the United Kingdom by:
Hay House UK Ltd, Astley House, 33 Notting Hill Gate, London W11 3JQ
Tel: +44 (0)20 3675 2450; Fax: +44 (0)20 3675 2451;
www.hayhouse.co.uk

Published and distributed in Australia by:
Hay House Australia Ltd, 18/36 Ralph St, Alexandria NSW 2015
Tel: (61) 2 9669 4299; Fax: (61) 2 9669 4144; www.hayhouse.com.au

Published and distributed in the Republic of South Africa by:
Hay House SA (Pty) Ltd, PO Box 990, Witkoppen 2068
info@hayhouse.co.za; www.hayhouse.co.za

Published and distributed in India by:
Hay House Publishers India, Muskaan Complex, Plot No.3, B-2,
Vasant Kunj, New Delhi 110 070
Tel: (91) 11 4176 1620; Fax: (91) 11 4176 1630; www.hayhouse.co.in

Copyright © 2016 by Belisa Vranich

Anatomical art by Hilary Mockewich; Exercise art by Maya Eilam

The moral rights of the author have been asserted.

A catalogue record for this book is available from the British Library.

ISBN: 978-1-78180-753-8

Printed and bound in Great Britain by TJ International Ltd, Padstow, Cornwall.

In memory of Liam Mikael Kowal.
Life is precious, please don't drink and drive.

CONTENTS

ACKNOWLEDGMENTS

To know even one life has breathed
easier because you have lived.
This is to have succeeded.
—*Ralph Waldo Emerson*

This book would never have seen the light of day without the vision of my literary agent, Peter McGuigan, of Foundry Media, and the inspiration of Senior Editor Daniela Rapp, of St. Martin's Press. To them I give heartfelt thanks for having the foresight and open-mindedness to understand the far-reaching significance of the inhale and exhale on the body, mind, and soul. To the Foundry team of Emily Brown, Kirsten Neuhaus, Alicka Pistek, Heidi Gall, and Claire Harris, and to the St. Martin's/Macmillan team of Brant Janeway, John Karle, Angelique Giammarino, Anne Marie Tallberg, Jessica Preeg, and Dori Weintraub, I express my deepest appreciation for their poignant feedback. I wish to acknowledge the contributions of those forward-thinking writers and journalists who covered this topic in its youth—Lisa Held, Carole Sabas, Sumathi Reddy, Cassie Shortsleeve, Marissa Stephenson, Jason Fine, Alix Strauss, Anna Maltby, Joshua David Stein, Drew Grant, Phyllis Korkki, Amy Maclin, and Alison Davis. I openly express my debt to

Vernick Alvarez for his steadfast friendship, even under grueling deadlines; to Max Smith for his patience in translating my impulsive e-mails; to Connor Mitchell for his modeling skills in the illustrations; to the capable artists Gerald Echeverria and Hilary Mockewich for their talent and remarkable flexibility.

Steve Kardian was a stalwart, unfaltering in his belief in *Breathe* from day one. Kellen Mori and Patricia Moreno were always there for me with their unfailing encouragement, as were Tricia Williams and Peder Regan with their unswerving support, and Jeff Burns of Sci Med Media with his time and valuable input. I would also like to thank my yoga teacher, Monica Jaggi, and my dependable assistant and sister-friend, Alyson Cook, without whom I'd be helplessly teaching on my own in California. Don Saladino, you have truly been my anchor in your generosity and friendship over this year. For their mentorship in business and friendship alike, I thank Melissa Hobley, Martin Lindstrom, Karrie Wolfe, and Corinne Pipitone.

Shirine Coburn, my friend, neighbor, and impromptu business mentor, I'm so lucky to have you in my life. Cesar Millan recognized the importance of breath in both man and dog, Serena Lee generously gave her legal advice and wit, and Henry "The Professor" Akins was unfailing in his encouragement and friendship. Earnest thanks are due to Adam Furman, Buddy and Renata at Saibot Media Inc.; my UK team, Caspian Dennis, Sandy Violette, Ben Fowler, Michelle Pilley, and Jo Burgess; and Kim and Denise of Bikram Yoga University Village. For their enduring encouragement throughout the year, I must express my gratitude to Shawn Perine, Sejal Patel, David Wallace, Robert Penzel, Social Diva Peg Samuel, Jen Widerstrom, and Hank Nation. To Tom Hermann and Agent Gregory Saunders, I deeply appreciate your understanding of the importance of breathing for endurance and stress management. I would also like to thank Joe March for his tenacity in bringing this part of health to light and, of course, David Elliot for introducing me to breathwork from its inception. Thank you, Caitlin Mitchell, for your unwavering friendship and generosity in helping this book to move forward and the classes to succeed. Dr. Amy Brown, your guidance and insight have been priceless. Rachel Ash, Dr. Anthony Lyon, Maureen Dodd, Dr. Stephanie Marango, Dr. Gabrielle Lyon, Dr. Jack Mantione: thank you so much for inviting me to be part of the team. I cannot close without recognizing the role of Sean Hyson, for coming along this path with me in so many ways—a veritable testament to our friendship.

BREATHE

INTRODUCTION

What if I said I had a medicine that would keep you calm but alert? That would relax and energize you? That would help you recover, boost your immune system, lower the oxidative stress that causes aging, power you up, and fuel every cell in your body, from your frazzled brain to your taxed muscles? You'd say, "Give it to me," right? Well, here it is. And no side effects. Take it every day—doctor's orders.

Life-changing? Yes, that's a word I keep hearing over and over from my clients. The first time, I thought it was an exaggeration. "Life-changing?" I cocked my head. "Yes, life-changing," they would insist, often after only the first session.

Teaching people to breathe is giving them the easiest "lifehack" ever—it fixes the problem (whether it's breathlessness, anxiety, pain, or acid reflux) from the bottom up, providing an immediate and almost confusing sense of relief. Changing your breathing truly does affect—immediately—the body, mind, and soul. And, most important, the impact takes place at both the cellular and the muscular levels.

You *know* your breathing could be better. Maybe it just gets "stuck" somewhere on the inhale, or you simply feel that you can never get enough air; or maybe you just sense in your gut that something isn't quite right. You know how good a big, relaxing sigh and a deep, deep breath feel, and you wish you could hold that sensation longer. You may not know the first thing about respiration and pulmonary medicine beyond the plastic torso you've seen in your pediatrician's office, or the poster for the Heimlich maneuver you've stared at while waiting for your food at your favorite take-out place, but the idea of "breathing better" resonates with you. However, it sounds daunting . . .

Your body wants to breathe in the way it was designed to: *in an anatomically congruous way*. Right now, it's not.

Think about that feeling of picking up something you once did well. Something you put aside because life got complicated and the years went by. You start out tentatively, feeling rusty, and then all of a sudden, the motor scooter balances, the piano keys all seem to be in the right place—and your body remembers.

My background as a clinical psychologist working with children led me to focus intently on *how* the information about breathing was presented in a learning situation. When someone says, "How come no one ever explained it this way?", usually with an expletive or two along the way, or "This is so easy but so game-changing," I know I have reached my goal.

I'm talking about life-changing concepts presented in simple, digestible language.

Breathing is the oldest, most basic thing we do every day of our lives. It's the first thing we must do when we are born, the thing we do most often until our last breath. Everyone breathes, regardless of age and country of origin. That's why the concept of teaching breathing seems so unusual, doesn't it? But when you recognize the extensive critical problems incorrect breathing has created, breathing the right way becomes mind-blowing. Simple but mind-blowing. Life-changing.

The very first step is to see *how* you breathe. Since you're already reading this book, it might be that you have a very, very specific reason for doing so: It could be a breathing disorder, after having smoked for years, or a feeling of anxiety and a sense that you breathe too fast, or maybe people keep telling you that you "don't seem to be breathing."

Just as in any appointment with an expert, when you come to see me, you have to talk about symptoms—but I want to know important details and nuances going all the way back to your childhood. I want to know about you because I truly believe that *you* are the expert on your own body. I'll follow with information, recommendations, and homework.

This might be the easiest and the most profound change you will ever make.

Easy? Yes, your body *wants* to breathe fully. And once you start, you may find yourself saying, "I can't stop thinking about my breathing" or "I'm almost obsessed with my breathing!" And it's due to the fact that our breathing has gotten so bad and the explanations feel so intuitively "right," that a lightbulb of understanding goes off. As a result, it's hard *not* to want to make some changes, even if they're small ones.

You might find you naturally remind yourself about your breathing throughout the day, or you might find that, the first week, you need some help from your electronics to remind you—or you might find that *bang*, you switch to a perfect breath, and never look back. You might find that you get so good at it, are so excited about it, that you use this knowledge to teach others when they're stressed or winded.

Research shows, and multimillion-dollar marketing companies know, that health behaviors are the hardest to change. Regardless of the threat or the prize, people often resist changing their ways when it comes to health habits. Yet changing the way people understand respiration and getting them to adjust to it has been oddly easy, and it's because of two simple things I repeat in class and throughout this book: *You used to breathe this way, and your body wants to breathe this way.*

This book is meant to be a primer, a first step toward something that somehow has been held as too complex, too natural, too elusive to explain in simple terms. I hope *Breathe* will inspire and catapult you to do more.

By the time you get to the end of this book you will have changed. How intense and how long-term the change will be is up to you, but I know that it will be impossible for you to read what I'm about to impart to you about breathing—in the way that I present it—and not become a healthier person. Even the teeniest change will be for the better; it will have a huge ripple effect on your mental and physical health, owing to the fact that healthy breathing is the foundation, the very cornerstone of health.

HOW THIS BOOK WORKS

You can't see your breathing, you can't see your lungs, and the deep muscles involved don't have a lot of nerve endings, so they're hard to feel. Relearning how to breathe, then, is very different than any other type of learning you may have attempted. In addition, in order to make a change, your demanding and fussy brain needs to understand the why, the how, and the where, in order to dismantle your previously acquired cognitive bias (that is, your bad habits). Here's what you can expect:

First, I'll give you a detailed explanation of how you breathe. It may seem a simple explanation, but it is not a simple process at all. My overarching mission has been to present complex information in a way that is easily digestible and intuitively *feels* right.

Then you'll get numbers and a grade, in order to know your baseline and be able to work from there. What this means is that you'll get to give your own particular style of breathing a name and will be able to understand what you do and why, and how you got there.

Moving on, you'll do a series of exercises until you find one that makes you go "Aha, I think I get it. This makes sense in a nonverbal way." Maybe you'll be lucky and there will be two or three exercises that feel oddly natural. You may have moments of it being so easy you wonder if you are in fact doing it correctly.

Then you'll catch yourself doing it wrong, grimace, and start again.

But then the moments of "being right" will happen more often, or get easier. You'll think you feel your body relax. You'll wonder if you're imagining it. (You won't be.)

What will be happening is that you'll be understanding:

- your breathing from multiple angles
- how your lifestyle has affected your breathing
- how to dismantle your bad habits
- how your health is being affected by bad breathing
- what to look for as you improve your breathing

It will be up to you to set up a workout, one that you do daily (maybe several times throughout the day). The pivotal part of success has to do with your assertively choosing a workout for yourself, noting your progress, and just as you would at the gym, adding a weight or a rep, once you're ready.

Have a notepad next to you. Underline, highlight, write in the margins.

Steps You'll Take While Using This Book

1. Grade yourself using the instructions that are detailed in chapter 2. Note your style of breathing and measure your Vital Lung Capacity. Use the baseline forms to log your symptoms at the start of this program and at the end of the fourteen days.

2. Make a workout for yourself exactly as you would with any exercise plan or weight-lifting routine at the gym. The baseline you have determined is the starting number. Make a commitment to focus on your lungs and breathing muscles every day for at least ten minutes. It doesn't matter if you're doing this to address stress, to get energized, or to get more oxygen to your muscles and

organs so you can sleep better, heal faster, or perform better. What does matter is that you treat your workout like a regimen for fourteen days.

3. Determine your "max." This may mean that you can do forty Exhale Pulsations before you can't do any more. Or it may mean that you can do your breathing count for two minutes before you get jumbled up or distracted. That's okay. As with any exercise, you need to know what your starting point and upper limits are and grow on that.

4. Don't get thrown by the idea that this is "just breathing." You're working out very important muscles in your body that have probably been idle. Feeling tired is the result we're looking for. You're working internal muscles, and there will be a moment where you hit your "max."

5. Treat the next fourteen days like a health commitment from which you cannot stray. Make adjustments in your life in order to be able to dedicate at least ten minutes a day to your workout. (While ten minutes is the minimum, if you're motivated and would like to do fifteen, go ahead.) If you'd like to do ten minutes twice, or three times a day, do it!

At some point over the next two weeks, your body will "remember" what it has to do. You'll notice that your brain feels less foggy, you'll know how to unwind at the end of the day, and whatever hurts in your body will be alleviated. You may find in a few months that you need to reread parts of the book and take things up a notch, maybe do the harder exercises. You have more power over how you feel than you realize. Taking control of your breathing will prove that to you.

Once this sinks in, don't resist the urge to "fix" your family and friends. Teaching someone else can help you gain even more mastery over this information.

1

DO YOU BREATHE, TOO?

You'd think that I'd introduced myself as a sex expert when I divulge that I teach breathing nowadays.[1] People get all excited, and I get railroaded with questions about breathlessness, smoking, breath-holding, high-altitude training, yoga breathing—the list goes on and on. Some ask questions because they have a strong hunch that something is wrong with their breathing.

Due to my having worked with a wide and varied population as a psychologist over the last twenty years, I handle diverse and elusive topics easily. I've conducted neuropsychological evaluations on seizure patients, worked with violent ex-convicts, with crack babies in the '80s, with emotionally disturbed, hearing-impaired French fifth-graders, with pro athletes, with stressed-out mothers-of-multiples, and with corporate CEOs. And guess what? Everybody breathes.

My knowledge about how the brain works, about child development, the significance of IQ, and the effects of psychopathology and trauma makes my analysis of your breathing something above and beyond a respiratory test at a hospital. In fact, all breathing tests can tell you is whether or not you're "within normal limits."[2] I do all the

---

1   In fact, I was at one time a health and sex editor at *Men's Fitness* magazine.
2   "Normal," right now, is not very healthy—it just means that you're within acceptable ranges. I am looking for *optimal*.

same tests, but then I do something only a professional who has studied personality and motivation can do: *I look at your style of breathing—where your breath is coming from*. Because while a test will measure your lung capacity, only a diagnosis of *how you breathe* can give you information on how it is affecting your emotional health, your posture, and—even more important, since it is a functional assessment—how it is affecting your life emotionally and physically, and, ultimately, how to fix it *without a prescription*.

Everybody breathes, and the breath affects everything. Everything. I've written this book so that you can find help for your anxiety, your sleeplessness, that sense of constriction around your chest, your irritable bowel. Breathing incorrectly may either have caused any one of these ailments or exacerbated it.[3] So working on your breathing should be part of the solution.

Nevertheless, rarely does the clinician you are seeing, whether it be your GP or your chiropractor, know to whom to send you in order to correct your breathing. And if they do give you a referral, that practitioner's style of teaching may be way too esoteric or way too technical to make sense to you.

How did we get so lost when it comes to something as basic as breathing? We know we can live for some time without water or food, but not without air. We know oxygen is critical, but our understanding of the *specifics* is poor. The time we dedicate to the health of our lungs and the efficiency of our breathing is usually nonexistent. While we give breathing lip service in songs and inspirational Facebook posts, we assume that efficient breathing just *happens*. Notwithstanding, our collective health has been getting worse and worse: increased blood pressure (*directly* affected by breathing), asthma attacks, panic attacks. Now we spend so much time just

---

3   See Michele M. Larzelere and Glenn N. Jones, "Stress and Health," *Primary Care: Clinics in Office Practice 35*, no. 4 (2008).

trying to plug up the dam that is our health that we've lost sight of the big picture, and especially of the fact that the strength of our breathing *muscles* and the balance of oxygen in our body are the cornerstones of our health.[4]

The human body can be very tough and resilient; it can work for a long time on one cylinder, limping around for decades. You can live taking in hamster-size breaths, but you'll suffer, your sleep will suffer, and so will your concentration, feeling of balance, and ability to perform. You'll be alive, but not a very happy hamster.

This book is very personal—it's about *your* breathing. And how you'll use this knowledge is very personal, too. Perhaps, after this, you'll teach your yoga class differently, go on to study different styles of meditation that seemed highly unlikely before, or solve your spouse's digestive problem and neck pain.

Or maybe you'll now nod knowingly when you hear Tony Robbins tout the importance of breathing or agree with Arianna Huffington when she does the same.[5] You might feel even more moved by Rocky's puffs of white exhale vapor as he runs atop of the steps of the Philadelphia Museum of Art, or hum along smugly with Pearl Jam's "Just Breathe," as if you know a secret others don't.[6]

So, your hunch that something was not quite right, is right. Most people are intuitive enough, when called on it, to know that something is wrong with their breathing. Or that their breathing could

---

4 Sheldon Saul Hendler, M.D., Ph.D., stresses the role played by breathing in maintaining good health and shows how proper breathing can help overcome aches and pains, exhaustion, asthma, and other ailments in his book *The Oxygen Breakthrough: 30 Days to an Illness-free Life*. As *Publishers Weekly* points out, "His 'breakthrough' focuses on a central but oft-forgotten fitness mechanism: proper breathing."

5 *The Sleep Revolution: Transforming Your Life, One Night at a Time*, especially Appendix B.

6 Or Pink Floyd's "Breathe" or Maroon 5's "Harder to Breathe," to name just a few.

Oxygen is sustenance in a way that food can never be. Yes, you should eat leafy greens, organic and local, and take your vitamins . . . but the best way to take care of yourself is to deal with the most important thing first: your breathing. Everything else is secondary.

be better. I repeat throughout the book that "breathing is something your body has done well before, and it is something that it wants to do well."

LET'S GO

You've probably heard some talk recently about breathing exercises. You may have brushed off the idea as trendy, but now there is a feeling that yes, yes, actually that *is* something you'd like to try. Though you don't know how, you do know in your gut that improved breathing could help you feel better. Still, even the term "better" is vague. Perhaps better breathing could energize you a little, rid you of the feeling of being tired all the time, or improve your memory. Maybe it could even help cut down the number of medications your doctor has prescribed. And maybe, just maybe, it could help you deal with the increasing stress in your life that—regardless of how many New Year's resolutions you devote to finding balance, taking time to relax, and being in the now—you can't get under control.

You shake your head and roll your eyes, but then you think, what if this *is* the magic bullet? What if something this simple can make you healthier?

You are right. Your intuition is right. Your instinct is right. Despite not being able to peer into your own chest, and knowing that the important stuff you inhale and exhale is totally invisible, I can say that you are absolutely 100 percent right. In fact, it can lessen pain and help you heal faster; help your digestive problems, be they acid reflux, irritable bowel, or constipation; lower your cortisol level, making for easier weight loss; and lower your blood pressure faster and more permanently than any medication on the market. You got it all right.

OXYGENATE FROM THE INSIDE OUT

Breathing: at first you might dismiss it as the stuff of pop songs, but once you realize that oxygen is body fuel at a cellular level—it's how you nourish your brain and muscles—well, it starts making sense. A lot of sense.[7]

And you do know this: you consider buying that face cream that professes to "oxygenate," you toy with the idea of taking supplements that promise increased oxygenation, and you drink alkaline water that promises to lower your acidity and oxygenate you better. So now consider something you could do just as quickly and more cheaply, merely by adjusting your inhale and exhale just a tad. After all, the goal of all the supplements you take, green juices you drink, and workouts you do is to oxygenate you better. So why not go to the source?

How well you breathe is the best indicator of how healthy you are and how long you'll live. "If I had to limit my advice on healthier living to just one tip," says Dr. Andrew Weil, "it would be simply to learn *how to breathe correctly.*"

The opposite is true as well, and even more extreme than you may realize: *"All* chronic pain, suffering, and disease are caused by a lack of oxygen at the cell level . . . Proper breathing nourishes the cells of the body with oxygen, and optimizes the functioning of the body on all levels," states the eminent Dr. Arthur C. Guyton.[8] So why hasn't this been evident to everyone? I'll give you three reasons:

---

7 Ever wonder about the composition of air? Just imagine sitting in a typical classroom (30 feet by 30 feet, with a 10-foot-high ceiling). Oxygen would cover the first 2 feet of the floor; nitrogen, the next 7 feet, 10 inches; argon would be a 1-inch layer; and the remaining gases would fill the last inch.

8 Dr. Guyton's *Textbook of Medical Physiology* was a basic book in medical schools for more than fifty years. John E. Hall first co-authored with the ninth edition in 1996. It is the world's bestselling physiology book.

1. You didn't realize you felt so crummy. Succinctly put, until you feel better, you don't realize how bad you were feeling before. Plus, you can't really see the damage that's taking place. For example: when your stomach doesn't feel good, the upset is pretty obvious in your bowel movements (or lack thereof). With breathing and oxygen, the results are widespread throughout your entire body; however, lack of oxygen isn't something that cries out for immediate attention or needs a visible bandage or crutch. The good news: the changes will be unquestionably evident after two weeks of doing the breathing exercises that I'm going to outline.

2. You got used to Band-Aids (and pills). Medical care usually makes us feel better right away with a pill, a shot, or surgery—but it doesn't go to the source of the problem. As a society, we're neither accustomed to nor taught to search for the root of the problem and solve it from there. Take blood pressure, for example: medication is highly effective, whereas breathing exercises are just as effective for lowering it without side effects by going to the source (in this case, overarousal of the sympathetic nervous system).

3. The change from the healthy breathing of a child to the dysfunctional breathing of an adult could creep in over the years. A bad fright in adolescence, for example, could change one's breathing from full to shallow. And this Shallow Breathing, reinforced by a hunched posture that is the result of years of sitting at a desk or driving, could become ingrained. A stressful event, followed by a back injury as a young adult, could lead to dysfunctional breathing, which becomes a habit after a few years; then stress and a culture of "gut-sucking" leads to sipping air haltingly, not exhaling completely, and never getting as much oxygen as is needed in order to think clearly and sleep well.

ONE STEP FORWARD, TWO STEPS BACK: WE HAVE EVOLVED, BUT OUR BREATHING HAS DEVOLVED

While our brains have gotten bigger and we have the potential to live to 120 and to break records in speed and capacity in sports every year, most of us breathe in a dysfunctional way. Our breathing has actually devolved over time. This is not to suggest that we are turning back into fish, but rather that our breathing has become incrementally inefficient in view of what it could be.

Why? We want everything fast: We walk faster than we did ten years ago, we eat faster, we communicate faster, and we actually age faster when exposed to oxidative stress for too long a time.[9] Acid reflux can even come from swallowing too fast, then jumping to the next task. We are under constant pressure to go to sleep quickly and to wake up quickly. And, consequently, what happens? Our breathing is constantly in "fast mode," shallow and quick, which in turn has terrible health repercussions.

You get it; it makes sense. Many illnesses are caused or made worse by a lack or imbalance of oxygen. Your system may be too acidic or inflammatory, or perhaps you're carrying stubborn pounds that won't come off because of high cortisol, or you're suffering from memory problems owing to an oxygen-starved brain. And yes, your energy level is low because you don't fuel your cells with the one thing that they need to make all those expensive organic foods and supplements digestible: oxygen. Every time you breathe, you nourish your body and brain. So why don't you start to feed them better? You can start now.

---

9   Antonino D. Romano et al., "Oxidative Stress and Aging," *Journal of Nephrology* 23, no. 15 (2010).

THE ULTIMATE ANSWER TO STRESS

By changing your breathing you will be able *to control stress—not let it control you.* How?

- By deactivating dysfunctional breathing patterns
- By realigning your breathing to work with your body, not against it
- By learning to activate your underutilized diaphragm muscle and working your breathing muscles, just as you would in physical therapy

DO THIS

Make sure you log in your baseline numbers for stress, pain, sleeplessness, fatigue, etc., at the end of this chapter. Observe how cumulative breathing exercises start to change your health overall, and then after fourteen days, fill out the forms in Appendix 3. Daily exercise makes a difference immediately in the short term as well. Keep notes for each of the fourteen days by using the pages provided at the end of this book.

CAN THIS BOOK REPLACE A BREATHING CLASS?

Yes! This book is organized in the same way my class is, with the same exercises and the same positive results. But, you may ask, what is a "breathing class" anyway? A breathing class is a modern, practical approach to an ancient healing art; it is an exercise class (you'll sweat!) for your lungs; it is a meditation-for-people-who-can't-

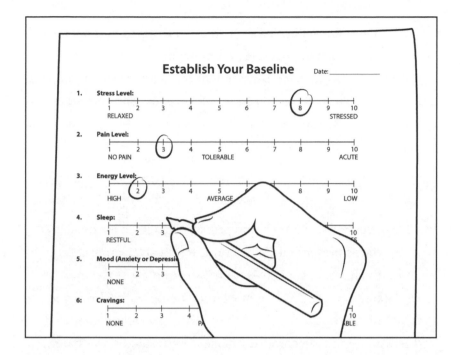

Establish Your Baseline   Date: _____

1. **Stress Level:**
   1   2   3   4   5   6   7   8   9   10
   RELAXED   STRESSED

2. **Pain Level:**
   1   2   3   4   5   6   7   8   9   10
   NO PAIN   TOLERABLE   ACUTE

3. **Energy Level:**
   1   2   3   4   5   8   9   10
   HIGH   AVERAGE   LOW

4. **Sleep:**
   1   2   3   10
   RESTFUL

5. **Mood (Anxiety or Depressi**
   1   2   3
   NONE

6: **Cravings:**
   1   2   3   4   10
   NONE   P   BLE

meditate class. It deals with anatomy and psychology, it can alleviate back pain, address your acid reflux, get you oxygenated faster and better than any medication. (Even for athletes, it is a secret weapon.[10] They don't need more cardio for their endurance; they need this book.) Breathing exercises can energize you better than a Red Bull and get you to sleep faster than an Ambien.

If you are going to make a New Year's resolution this year, let it be retraining yourself to breathe in a way that nourishes your body *at a cellular level.*

Whether this is the start of a whole new mind/body makeover or you just want a full night's sleep, a satisfying deep breath, or better endurance, you actually do have the solution within you. Your hunch that your breathing is important was right on target.

Where you go from here is up to you. Make it life-changing.

---

10 See "How to Breathe and Exhale," about my work with martial artists, in the February 2016 issue of *Jiu-Jitsu* magazine.

It was funny how I really had to understand that my breathing was in a completely separate part of my body, not up by my head. And like Dr. Belisa said, it's cluttered up there (in my head). Breathe better and you'll feel like you have more space, and are more balanced. It made me chuckle that it actually made sense once I was doing it right. —Liam, age 29

Paul's Story

At age thirty-five, Paul's blood pressure had risen inexplicably and he was prescribed medication. Paul had been muscular in his twenties, but due to a back injury, he'd lost the muscle and gained weight. While he blamed being out of breath on a lack of cardio, the truth was that the extra weight had caused his diaphragm to become immobile. As a result, he was barely exhaling and retaining stale residual air. All this became a self-perpetuating cycle of unhealthy factors and mild depression—which showed in his angry and cynical disposition.[11] Paul's main motivation was to get off the blood-pressure medication, and once I showed him how he could see the numbers fall on the blood pressure monitor with his breathing alone, he was a believer. The next time he saw his doctor, his blood-pressure medication was reduced. The trickle-down effect of empowerment gained momentum: the herniated disc pain in his back grew much milder. He understood how to breathe in order to help his spine and to relax his back muscles. As a side effect, Paul found he was able to lose weight and use the meditation/breathing as a way to deal with his depression effectively.

---

11 Often men feel irritability more than sadness when suffering from depression.

This book, then, is about relearning how to breathe—a breath where the lungs hug and release the heart lovingly, aid in the rhythm and muscle movement of digestion, and really just let the body do what it is supposed to, what it wants to do.

BASELINE NUMBERS

1. Stress: On a scale of 1 to 10, with 10 being the most stress, how stressed are you now? Over the past week, what was your average stress level? Over the last month? Don't judge your stress by the event that caused it. Stress can be caused by worries about an impending problem, not necessarily the result of a direct trauma. This is a subjective number that has to do only with you. Over the next fourteen days, rate your stress.

2. Pain: If you're experiencing pain of any type, from fibromyalgia to back pain, rate your pain as well. A rating of 1 is no pain, 5 is average (tolerable), 10 is acute. As with #1 above, don't judge whether your pain "deserves" a certain number or should be higher or lower; simply rate it by the way it feels to you—regardless of whether you have a high or low pain threshold.

3. Energy level: While your energy level may fluctuate throughout the day, rate your level on an average, as compared to prior days. Start by noting how you remember feeling last week and the previous month. Rate each day with a number for the next fourteen days.

4. Sleep: If you under-breathe, it's quite possible that your sleep is affected. Do you have difficulty going to sleep or staying asleep? If you have trouble "turning off the chatter"—the running commentary in your head that keeps you up at night—rate

how severe your sleep problems are.[12] If you take medication to help get you to sleep, rate this problem a 10.

5. Mood: Rate your mood last week, and last month. If you've had specific changes in your mood (depression or anxiety), note when they started and record any fluctuations in severity. Then, every day over the next two weeks, measure your mood. Remember that a higher number means a severe increase in your depression or anxiety. A 1 or 2 would be a very good day, with little or no symptoms of depression or anxiety, while a 10 would be one where you would consider seeking ER care.

6. Cravings: If weight loss is an issue with you, give your feelings of hunger or cravings a number. Again 1 is none, while 10 is intolerable. Note your history with feelings of hunger and cravings over the last month, and the last year in general. Note the time of the craving and type of food you craved as well.

7. Describe and rate your neck and shoulder stiffness/discomfort.

8. Describe and rate your sense of mental clarity and memory.

9. Describe and rate any problems with your digestion, including not emptying your bowels once a day, acid reflux/heartburn, irritable bowel syndrome. Include any pelvic-floor problem; e.g., light leakage, incontinence, or urgency, if it's applicable.

10. Endurance: Rate your endurance, whether it be when going up a set of stairs you take every day or a five-mile run several times a month. Factor in your energy level, and strive to get a clear sense of how your endurance changes as you do these exercises over the next few days. The number, in this case, is very subjective and should reflect how you assess your conditioning (ability to catch your breath).

---

12 Anxiety will cause you to have low GABA, which means your mind will continue to race at night. High cortisol and low progesterone are also common culprits.

Establish Your Baseline

DATE: _____

1. Stress Level:

0	1	2	3	4	5	6	7	8	9	10
RELAXED										STRESSED

2. Pain Level:

0	1	2	3	4	5	6	7	8	9	10
NO PAIN					TOLERABLE					ACUTE

3. Energy Level:

0	1	2	3	4	5	6	7	8	9	10
HIGH					AVERAGE					LOW

4. Sleep:

0	1	2	3	4	5	6	7	8	9	10
RESTFUL					AVERAGE					RESTLESS

5. Mood (Anxiety or Depression):

0	1	2	3	4	5	6	7	8	9	10
NONE					TOLERABLE			VERY DEPRESSED/ANXIOUS		

6: Cravings:

0	1	2	3	4	5	6	7	8	9	10
NONE				PASSING CRAVINGS					INTOLERABLE	

7: Neck and Shoulder Stiness/Discomfort:

0	1	2	3	4	5	6	7	8	9	10
NONE								INTENSE DISCOMFORT		

8. Mental Clarity and Memory:

0	1	2	3	4	5	6	7	8	9	10
EXCELLENT								DIFFICULTIES REMEMBERING		

9: Problems with Digestion (constipation, irritable bowel, acid reux, etc.):

0	1	2	3	4	5	6	7	8	9	10
NONE					TOLERABLE				SEVERE PROBLEMS	

10: Endurance (self-determined measure):

2

HOW BAD IS IT, DOC?

WORRIED? YOU SHOULD BE

Poor breathing puts you at higher risk for a slew of diseases and problems.[13] Which one (or more) of these resonates with you?

- *Cognitive problems.* Unbalanced oxygen and a stress-inducing style of breathing make concentration difficult and cause problems with memory (and can even change your brain).
- *Emotional health.* Both depression and anxiety are worsened by shallow, erratic breathing.
- *Pain.* Whether it's injury pain or fibromyalgia, if it hurts and you breathe badly, it's going to hurt more (and longer).

> How you breathe is an indicator of your longevity and quality of life. The health of your body is reflected in the way you breathe. Change the way you breathe, and there will automatically be positive changes in your longevity and quality of life.

---

13 The renowned Framingham study, which has followed the health of 5,209 men and women and their descendants over three generations, presents persuasive evidence that the most significant factor in health and longevity is *how well one breathes*. The complete study can be accessed at the National Institute of Health's database: http://www.ncbi.nlm.nih.gov/pubmed/.

- *Back issue.* Whether it's a cervical spine, lower back, or neck and shoulders issue, if you aren't breathing well, it's directly affecting your spine health.

- *Low energy.* Bad breathing lessens the body's ability to deliver oxygen to the cells. The cells get stressed and have to prioritize survival over growth.

- *Hypertension.* Suboptimal breathing may contribute to hypertension. When you breathe badly, the blood vessels constrict, which can lead to higher blood pressure, and which in turn makes the heart work harder. In effect, people with high blood pressure who were made to breathe slower several minutes a day saw their blood pressure drop.[14]

- *Acidity.* Faster breathing results in respiratory alkalosis. This, in turn, snowballs into a slew of medical disorders that can be long-term and serious.

- *Digestive woes.* Optimally, your breathing muscles stimulate peristalsis, the wavelike motion of the intestines that promotes digestion and elimination. Without this internal abdominal massage, you're likely to find yourself coping with issues such as constipation, bloating, gas, heartburn, and irritable bowel syndrome.

- *Sleep.* You've been breathing in a way that tells your neurological system that you are in "fight or flight" all day. There's no way you're going to just switch into gentle deep sleep immediately. Period.

---

14 For more specifics, go to http://www.ncbi.nlm.nih.gov/pubmed/10205248/ and http://www.ncbi.nlm.nih.gov/pmc/articles/PMC2288755/.

You might not think much about your lungs until you're short of breath or have a condition like asthma that affects their function. But these seemingly ordinary organs have the power to determine whether or not you're supplying your brain and body with the sustenance they need. The very purpose of the lungs is to draw in oxygen and remove carbon dioxide from your body. And keeping this balance is exactly what your body needs to be alert, productive, and happy.

IT'S NOT JUST ABOUT CARDIO

You find yourself gasping for air after climbing a few flights of stairs and automatically think, "I really need to do more cardio." It's true that cardio—or aerobic exercise—is crucial in keeping you healthy. It's a type of activity that can strengthen your heart muscle by improving its ability to pump blood (and oxygen) throughout the body. Cardio can have a bevy of benefits, *but your heart can only move as much oxygen as you bring into your body.* Here's the crux of the problem: cardio exercise gives your heart a great workout, but it does nothing to beef up the power of your lungs, improve the flexibility of your thoracic cavity (the bones, tendons, cartilage, and muscles that make up the chest wall), or strengthen your inspiratory (inhale) and expiratory (exhale) muscles and the thoracic diaphragm. In other words, you can have the heart and cardiovascular system of an elite athlete but the lungs and breathing muscles of a total couch potato. Just because you train until you're sweating up a storm and heaving for breath doesn't mean you're actually working out the specific components that make for better breathing.

OXYGEN IS CELL FUEL

Stop and consider how much money you spend on vitamins, juices, and the newest electrolyte-infused alkaline-neutral water. However, what it comes down to when all is said and done is that your body's main source of energy is *oxygen*. Period. As oxygen circulates throughout your system, it is released into the cells in your tissues and organs, where it can interact with certain enzymes, creating fuel for your body. Oxygen, then, is vital for the respiration and growth of healthy cells—the very cells that allow you to think, the cells that break down your food, the cells that produce balancing hormones and neurotransmitters. Without those hardworking cells, you'll find yourself reaching for energy drinks and medications to help you feel better. Meanwhile, the real solution is right under your nose.

Sure enough, it seems that everyone has a solution for increasing oxygen in the body, from mouth devices that restrict airflow, oxygen tents, and chlorophyll drops, to drinking ionized water or huffing canned oxygen. On the market, you'll also find supplements promising to improve the ability of red blood cells to bind with oxygen. While some have validity, others don't, so consider this: You can most certainly add oxygen to your blood, but the boost it gives you—if it does—is fleeting. Why not simply improve the way you breathe? And if you're breathing wrong all the time, shouldn't the first step be to correct this?

Imagine needing only two breaths instead of ten in order to catch your breath. *And* being able to push yourself more during your workouts and recover more quickly afterward. *And* your energy levels will naturally be higher. *And* you'll be able to think more clearly and recall more precisely. That's the promise of optimal oxygen intake—and it's something you can achieve by working out your breathing muscles.

A BETTER WAY TO BOOST OXYGEN

There is a better way to boost oxygen intake—and I'll teach it to you. Moreover, its effects are permanent (and free).

If you've ever seen cadaver studies of lungs, you must have been amazed at how far these organs can stretch (and if you haven't, head on over to YouTube right now for some mind-blowing images). The fact is, people use very little of all that lung space. That's because they are lazy breathers—taking short, shallow breaths from the chest, filling only the very top portion of the lungs with air. Then they do not exhale fully (with most breaths, 30 percent of stale air stays in the body). A rigid, inflexible thoracic cavity and rib cage, plus poor posture, also contribute to sluggish breathing.

The good news? While your parents (or, more accurately, their genes) are responsible for the size of your lungs, that doesn't mean you can't pump up their power. Let's take the first step right now.

DETERMINING YOUR BASELINE

Improving your breathing is the same as working out any other part of your body. You have a baseline and you work up from there.

Hate math? Just remember that the difference between your inhale and exhale (whether it's 1 inch, 2 inches, or 3) *should* be more than your exhale when you put a decimal between the first and second numbers. So if your exhale is 42 inches, then we're talking 4.2. If your exhale is 25 inches, then we're talking 2.5.

Just because you can't see your lungs working or can't see the air that comes in and goes out of them doesn't mean you can't measure your progress. In fact, it's critical that you do. I'll help you determine your baseline. Vital Lung Capacity (VLC) and breathing style are the two factors we're going to look at.

1. Vital Lung Capacity (VLC): Wrap a measuring tape an inch beneath your sternum.[15]

---

15 An early description of this method for measuring VLC appeared in 1852 in Dr. Henry Ancell's *A Treatise on Tuberculosis*: "One method is, to measure the

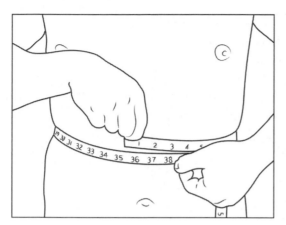 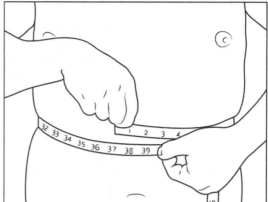

Your sternum (breastbone) is a long, flat, bony plate shaped like a capital "T" that connects to your rib bones via cartilage. You may feel a "notch" where your ribs curl up and meet in the very middle of your chest. Exhale and measure the circumference of your body. Then inhale and measure. Don't change the way you breathe in order to make this number change; simply breathe the way you do normally.[16] Subtract the exhale from the inhale, then divide that number (using a calculator) by the exhale. The result is your VLC, as a percentage.

2. Breathing style: The two overarching styles are *Vertical* and *Horizontal*. Most people are Vertical Breathers (also called

---

mobility of the walls of the chest, since this corresponds very closely with the actual breathing power. This may be done with a common tape measure. Firstly, the minimum circumference of the chest over the nipples, after a forced expiration; and secondly, the maximum circumference, after causing the chest to be fully expanded, should be noted . . . This method enables us to form a rough estimate of the vital capacity of the lungs, and I have found it practically useful" (p. 90).

16 For a visual on measuring VLC, check out chiropractor Dr. Paula Moore's video at http://www.youtube.com/watch?v=8G-HVCOYTGw.

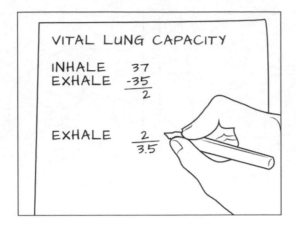

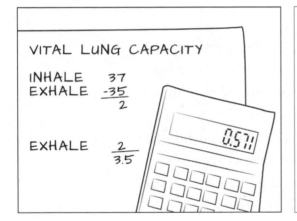

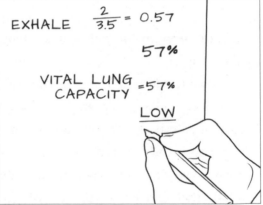

"Clavicular Breathers").[17] If you are a Vertical Breather, the following sentences will resonate with you:

- I feel as if I get taller when I inhale and shorter (or "come down") when I exhale.
- My shoulders move up when I inhale and down when I exhale.
- I feel as if I breathe "filling up": my whole body stretches slightly up when I inhale, then drops on the exhale.

---

17 They are also sometimes called "Apical Breathers." Go to http://collegeofmassage.com/Toronto/2013/05/apical-breathing for more on the subject.

- When I put one hand on my chest and one on my belly, *the top moves more.*
- When looking in the mirror, I see my neck "engage" on the inhale, then relax on the exhale.
- On the inhale, I try to think of the top of my head as lengthening upward, then coming down when I exhale. My middle stays still.
- I feel as if I breathe "up" when I inhale, and relax "down" when I exhale.

If, on the other hand, you are a Horizontal Breather, you'll identify with the following:

- My shoulders and neck stay completely still when I inhale. Nothing on the top of my body is involved at all in my breathing.
- Only my middle expands in all directions from under my pecs to my pelvis.
- I don't feel as if I get taller or lengthen when I breathe. If anything, I feel as if I move "out," then contract.
- My inhale feels like an expansion of my body horizontally, while my exhale feels as if I get thinner. No up and down at all.

More common than Horizontal Breathing is *Mixed Breathing.*

- I feel a little Vertical and a little Horizontal.
- Both my bottom and top hands move when I breathe: specifically, my top hand goes upward and my bottom hand moves outward.[18]

---

18 If your belly moves inward, this doesn't count as expanding belly movement; see "Paradoxical Breather" in Chapter 3.

Lourdes's Story

At seventeen years of age, Lourdes was brought in to see me by her parents because she had been diagnosed with acid reflux and irritable bowel syndrome. She was on the brink of hospitalization and had almost no energy at all, having been put through a bevy of invasive gastrointestinal tests. In passing, one doctor recommended that she learn diaphragmatic breathing. Frustrated that none of the doctors at the hospital could recommend a specialist to teach breathing, much less diaphragmatic breathing, her mother finally found me on the Internet. Because of my expertise as a psychologist, I was able to determine that Lourdes's anxious personality had manifested as a digestive problem, including very Vertical Breathing with little Vital Lung Capacity. Learning to use her diaphragm to breathe, along with calming breath exercises solved both problems at once. Lourdes gained weight back over the next four months and developed a daily breathing and meditation practice that helped control both her anxiety and her digestive problems.

GRADING

The Short Breathing IQ (BIQ) considers two very important parameters: your Vital Lung Capacity, as it's measured from the outside of your body, and your breathing style. Take a look at this grading chart. On the vertical axis, locate where you are as far as your style is concerned; and on the horizontal axis, find where your VLC is. (If you need a refresher when you do the division needed to get a percentage, see pages 26–28.)

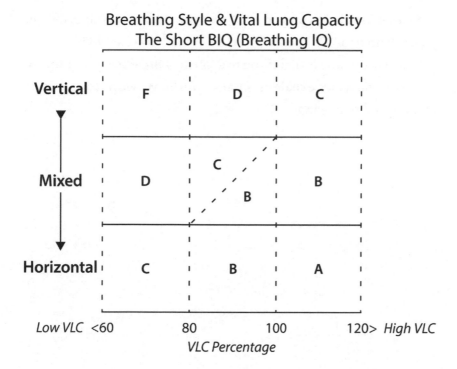

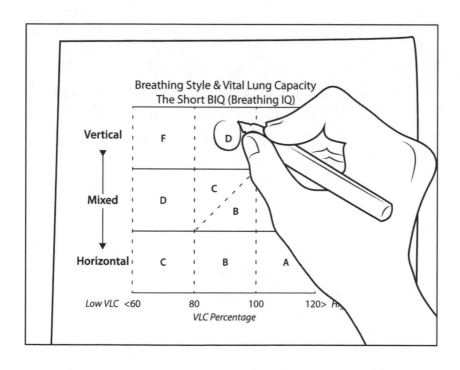

Does it look as if you got a "D" this time? Start working and get yourself up to a "C," then a "B," then an "A." You can do it!

The bottom line is that if you're a Vertical Breather—your inhale isn't big and your exhale is small—you have work to do. Start reading and practicing!

3

YOU'VE GOT IT ALL WRONG

Maybe too much inhaling, maybe not enough exhaling, maybe breathing way too fast. Due to any number of factors, very few people breathe to their full potential. I see this time and time again in the breathing classes I teach. A new client comes to me and reports that she's eating clean, drinking more water, popping supplements, seeing the chiropractor, and using a heating pad to keep old injuries at bay while icing new ones. She's doing everything right.

Then I ask her one simple question: *"How is your breathing?"* And she points to her nose and tells me about her allergies.[19]

I'm sure you can relate. But did you know that just about anything and everything—from your age, to your health history, to your texting addiction—can have a powerful impact on your capacity to breathe optimally? In this chapter, I'd

It speaks volumes that we all know what "fight or flight" is but we don't know its opposite. Do you? It's "rest and digest." In order to live a healthy life, you need both. Right now, most people stay in "fight or flight," as if they don't have an alternative. No wonder they can't sleep and have so many digestive problems: not enough "rest and digest."

---

19 For an easy read on everything you ever wanted to know about noses, check out http://care.american-rhinologic.org/nasal, especially the article about nasal physiology by Jeremiah Alt, M.D., and Noam Cohen, M.D.

like you to assess how you actually breathe and to consider the possibility that you're not breathing as well as you should—in everyday life, on the treadmill, at the computer.

SELF-EXAM: LET'S LOOK AT YOU

What's messing up your breathing? See if you answer *yes* to any of the following questions I ask my clients:

1. Do you sit in front of a computer or in a car or truck for work?
2. Do you wear compression garments, belts, support pantyhose, or a bulletproof vest?
3. As a child, did you live with any type of fear, anxiety, or worry over a period of time, even if you think you weren't traumatized by it?
4. Do you text throughout the day?
5. Do you carry a bag, knapsack, or purse? How much does it weigh?
6. Have you ever had pneumonia or recurring bouts of bronchitis?
7. Have you ever smoked or lived with a smoker?
8. Have you ever lived or spent time in a city with high levels of smog or pollution, or lived someplace with noxious smells?
9. Do you have a deviated septum or do you snore?
10. Do you have or have you ever had neck, shoulder, or back injuries?

Oh, and are you over the age of twenty-nine?[20]

How many questions did you say *yes* to? Even just one of these can lead to under-breathing, either by impairing lung function or

---

20 Yup, even your age affects your breathing. It might be said that things improve with time, but lung function isn't one of them—it naturally heads downhill after age twenty-nine.

laying the foundation for one or more of the abnormal breathing patterns to be discussed later in this chapter. If you're breathing poorly—and you probably are—you could be doing so for any number of reasons, apart from those mentioned in the quiz. These may include:

Chronic stress, anxiety, or a history of panic attacks or other anxiety disorders. Before you dismiss these as "not me," think about whether you've ever stayed awake worrying about money, your health, the stress of a divorce or breakup, your kids, or being the caretaker of elderly parents. If any one of these sounds familiar, chances are you're stressed out.

Technology and poor posture. Think your posture is fine? How many times a day do you bend your head to text, to update your Facebook status, or to play a game on your phone? How many hours are you hunched over a laptop or desk? These positions put your head and shoulders into a position that impairs breathing and, consequently, your health.[21]

Long periods of time spent sitting down, whether while driving, working, or watching TV. The latest studies of how many hours people sit a day report an average of thirteen hours.[22]

---

21 I address posture and FHP (Forward Head Posture) and their deleterious effects on breathing and health in detail in Chapter 7.

22 Check out http://www.prnewswire.com/news-releases/new-survey-to-sit -or-stand-almost-70-of-full-time-american-workers-hate-sitting-but-they-do-it -all-day-every-day-215804771.html.

You *used* to breathe right: Ask most five-year-olds to inhale and they expand their bellies without thinking twice. Ask most ten-year-olds, and the beautiful, perfect Horizontal Breath has disappeared: they'll mimic a dysfunctional adult Vertical Breath. What happened? Someone teased them about their belly and they started the habit of gut-sucking. Then came the visit to the doctor, when a stethoscope was put on their upper chest and they were asked to breathe (ah, the lungs must be there, no?). They started sitting—a lot. Maybe they took a tumble that led to some kind of torso pain . . . and the combination of all these changes, encouraged by adult modeling of bad breathing, left them over-using their shoulders and underusing their diaphragm to breathe.

Anything around your torso: a sports bra or just your average waistband that holds your pants or skirt around your middle.

Lung or nose issues. Broken nose, allergies or sinus problems, asthma, emphysema, and other respiratory diseases.

Your body. Beer belly, extra abdominal weight.

ABNORMAL BREATHING PATTERNS

Pause a moment and pay attention to your breath without trying to influence it. Now think about how you breathe in more challenging situations; e.g., during a workout or a jog. Are you using the right muscles to breathe? Are you filling just part of your lungs with oxygen-rich air? Chances are you're stuck in one of the following abnormal breathing patterns. In the last chapter, you noted whether you were a Horizontal or Vertical Breather (breathing up and down or widening when you inhale and exhale). Now look more specifically: Which of the following types sound familiar?

1. *Paradoxical Breather (Gasper).* Also known as "Reverse Breathing," this pattern uses your muscles in a contradictory manner; this is

to say, you draw your belly in during an inhale and relax it out during an exhale—the polar opposite of what you should be doing. Paradoxical Breathers take in significantly less air than anyone else, actually going against what their body wants to do, anatomically, with each inhale and exhale. Theory says that it comes from anxiety in childhood—try gasping in fear and see how you mimic that breathing.[23]

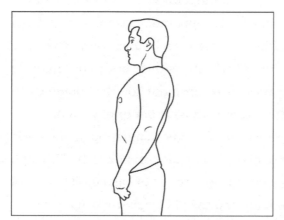
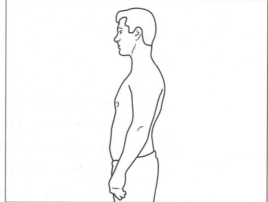

2. *Breath-Holder* (or *Periodic* or *Hypoxic Breather*). Periodically, throughout the day, you pretty much act as if you are under water. You hold your breath for seemingly no reason, and don't notice except when it gets pointed out to you that you yawn and sigh a lot (or that you don't seem to be breathing when you work out). This is another stress-fueled pattern. If you find this happening when you're at your computer, it's colloquially called "e-mail apnea."

---

23 When you startle an infant, his head, shoulders and hands will instinctively come up as his diaphragm sucks in. This is the startle response—or "Condition Red"—that is the body's instinctive way of preparing for whatever happens next. The problem is that most of us live in this ready state, breathing shallowly from our chests, explains Lieutenant Colonel David Grossman, who has trained Navy SEALs, British SAS soldiers, Green Berets, and federal agents. He is the author of the Pulitzer Prize–nominated book *On Combat*.

Due to the increased prevalence of Breath-Holders and No-Halers, I don't focus on breathing rates owing to the fact that they're hard to gauge correctly. All Vertical Breathers breathe too fast in general, since their breaths are smaller and less efficient than those of Horizontal Breathers. The general rule: Slower is better.

This is caused by a predatory, stress-induced type of concentration while at the screen (a type of concentration that has the focused intensity of a hunter stalking prey).

This abnormal pattern is alarmingly common. My clients have reported being surprised to find themselves holding their breath for several seconds throughout the day for no apparent reason. This pattern throws whatever balance they may have out of whack, as their body continuously tries to compensate for the moments in which they're not letting carbon dioxide out or oxygen in.

3. *Over-Breather (hyperventilating)*. Chronic ventilation at low levels results in an imbalance of carbon dioxide and oxygen. Although you're breathing more quickly, you're out of balance. The rate of breathing here is too high, and the pH levels are usually abnormal as well. There are two breakdowns here: your exhale is strong and your inhale is constricted, or the opposite—your inhale is long and your exhale is short.

4. *No-Haler*.[24] No inhale, no exhale; this breather just "hovers," sipping in air then barely letting it out. Your body doesn't expand and contract, it barely moves at all. These people tend to brace their bodies and make very little movement at all, saying their breath feels stuck in both directions.

Now that you know the many different types of abnormal breathing patterns and the factors that can influence how you breathe,

24 This is the term employed by Washington, D.C.–based martial arts and self-defense expert Thong Nguyen (personal correspondence).

you can see why virtually no adult these days breathes optimally without proper training.

As a last part of your assessment, I want you to rank some of the health problems you have so that you can see how they change over the next two weeks, and into the future. Whether it's your stress level, quality of sleep, back or neck pain, or digestion, give yourself a numerical rating on the sheet at the very back of this book. Keeping track of your progress makes learning—and sustaining your changes—easier.

I know what you're thinking: *Okay, so my breathing is terrible! Now what?* Well, now I'm going to show you why abnormal breathing patterns don't have to be "normal" for you—and how you can make every breath count.

Watch any resting animal breathe, and you'll witness the perfect breath: rhythmic, efficient, with the belly expanding and contracting. Young children, though still developing postural muscles, will usually breathe low in their bodies, using their diaphragms. Yet very few people sustain that Lower-body Breath to adulthood. Bad posture, injury, and just plain laziness lead them to the mediocre-at-best breathing they practice now. In essence, they're breathing the way our ancestors did when they were faced with fear, anxiety, or other *temporary* situations. Unfortunately, we've transformed these short-term solutions into long-term abnormal breathing patterns.

I had to laugh at myself. I've been breathing the opposite of most people, the opposite of the way my body is supposed to breathe, for as long as I know. It took a minute for me to understand that, but if I breathe with the muscle that's supposed to be my breathing muscle, my diaphragm, it makes sense. On the inhale, it should be helping my middle, where the best part of my lungs are, to expand. Duh! Meanwhile, all this time I've been squeezing the poor thing shut! And vice versa. While I've heard and understood that a belly breath is good for you, I've never had enough understanding or motivation to change my breathing. Now I do. It's frustrating as hell, but by day five it's getting a tiny bit easier every day. Especially when I tip back and start with the exhale. It's funny how my brain now understands, and it's just my body that has to get with it. But I figure if it takes two or three weeks, even a month, that's okay. It's worth it. I've been breathing wrong for decades; this is an important change and I'm going to do it. Funny enough, it's like I have no choice—and now that I know the why, I'm determined.—Marty, age 40

Mary's Story

At age seventy-six, Mary had been diagnosed with COPD (Chronic obstructive pulmonary disease) and came to The Breathing Class as a last resort. She was quick to list all the specialty breathing clinics she'd attended and how infuriating and perplexing it was to have a disorder often related to smoking when she'd never smoked a day in her life. Mary's style of breathing was significant: she was a Paradoxical Breather; i.e., she pulled in her middle on the inhale and then relaxed it on the exhale, all the while working against her diaphragm. Due to her using her neck and shoulders to breathe, she also had intense neck and shoulder pain, which she had just assumed was something she had to live with. The first step was to have her understand how she was working against her anatomy, and why this might have happened sometime between childhood and young adulthood. Finding the analogy and movements that made the change click and made sense to her both intellectually and kinesthetically was my goal. Mary had to understand and experience a "good breath," one she hadn't had in decades, in order to be able to change. The sessions paid off: seeing the numbers on the spirometer and her Vital Lung Capacity improve fed her motivation. She's back to walking on a daily basis and continues to raise the bar for the next goal for herself and her health with each appointment.

4

ACTIVATE AND RELEARN

You've seen those ads for antihistamines or air fresheners in which a model spreads her arms wide, twirling in a circle, and, expanding her chest, takes a deep, deep breath, and sighs blissfully. In another scenario, a coach will tell an athlete to breathe deeply. In most cases, the shoulders either move back or up. Unfortunately, this upper chest or Clavicular Breathing is not efficient; it uses only the smaller top part of your lungs, and that means that your diaphragm, which should be your main breathing muscle, is completely still. Bad, bad breathing.

Now, put one hand on your belly and one hand by your collarbones. Open your mouth, close your eyes, and take a couple of breaths. *Notice which hand moves.* Is your top hand moving up and down slightly, or is your bottom hand moving forward and back? Maybe you aren't sure of the direction, but you do know that one hand is moving more than the other. Or perhaps they're both moving, just a little bit. Ask someone to watch you breathe as you focus on

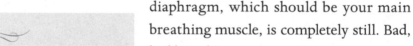

This isn't really a brand-new skill you have to learn; you used to do it right. It's just about remembering. Don't worry; you don't have to put breathing on that endless list of to-do's that require breaking down an old habit or painfully reminding yourself daily about a new one. It's simply about moving your breath down to the lower part of your body, where it used to be. Where it should be.

something else. Are they seeing one hand move more than the other? Or is it a combination of belly *and* upper chest movement?

MEET YOUR DIAPHRAGM

The most important and underappreciated muscle in your body is the diaphragm.[25] If you've heard about the diaphragm, you may have the misguided idea that only singers use it when reaching for a high "C," and that's about it. In fact, this large, pizza-size muscle plays an integral role in respiration. When you're not breathing with your diaphragm—and consequently not using the rest of your breathing muscles to their full potential—you're breathing just enough to survive, *but not enough to thrive.*

In the simplest terms, when you breathe properly—from the belly—your diaphragm flattens and spreads (see figures 1 and 2 on the following page), and your bottom ribs and abdomen push out. Often the tired-can't-breathe sensation you may have experienced is due to those very muscles fatiguing; however, since the sensation is not as specific as the burn in your calves or biceps when you're working out at the gym, you don't recognize it as signaling under-developed breathing muscles.

Got neck or shoulder pain?

When you're breathing through the top of your body, you're using neck and shoulder muscles that aren't meant to be primary breathing muscles. Hence, no matter how many massages you have, how many therapeutic pillows or ergonomic chairs you buy, you'll continue to have neck and shoulder discomfort until you change your breathing back to the right way. The good news: once you change your breathing, your neck and shoulder stiffness will get better, and stay better.

---

25 For an excellent article on the diaphragm by chiropractor Robert "Skip" George, see: http://www.dynamicchiropractic.com/mpacms/dc/article.php?id=55951.

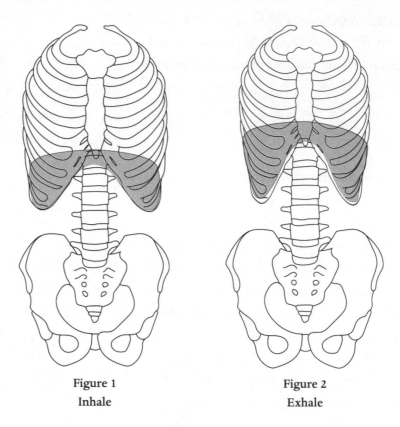

Figure 1
Inhale

Figure 2
Exhale

However, the diaphragm is just one major player in the game plan of breathing correctly. It's smack in the center of your body, surrounded and supported by the *erector spinae, transverse abdominis,* and pelvic-floor muscles. Your intercostals are also integral to respiration, while your outer core—the *rectus abdominus, quadratus lumborum,* and oblique muscles—help control your posture and movement. Strong breathing is a lot more than just the size of your lungs!

When your diaphragm and other specific breathing muscles aren't as strong as they should be, your breathing suffers. In fact, right now these muscles are probably downright weak. Not to worry, though: I'm going to challenge you to work your diaphragm and core as you never have before—and all without lifting a dumbbell or doing a single crunch.

RELEARN HOW TO BREATHE—SWITCHING BACK TO LOWER-BODY BREATHING (LBB)

As you just learned, chest-based breathing doesn't use all of the real estate in the lungs; moreover, it keeps you from drawing in the oxygen you need for energy, in order to be productive, to heal, and to sleep well at night.

So how does one go from a perfectly breathing infant to a poorly breathing adult? Well, as people get older, they sit for hours at desks, on sofas, on trains, and in cars—and these sustained postures can lead to bad breathing habits. Being worried, anxious, or scared can affect you, too. Plus, in a quest for flatter abs, many people tend to suck in their stomach, which forces them to breathe from the chest, not the belly. Not to be forgotten are back or shoulder injuries, which can compromise breathing even after they heal.

The goal is straightforward: *Relearn how to breathe by moving the breathing back down to the lower part of your body, where it belongs.* Okay, maybe getting there is not quite so simple, but when you determine which muscles to use and how to make them as strong as possible, you'll see results quickly. The fact is, the best breathing happens from your chest down. The bottom part of your ribs moves, your belly expands, your sides expand, and eventually, even your back expands.

BELLY BREATHING

Belly breathing is the introductory breath that gets you to breathe from the lower part of your body. *When you jut your belly out, you discover the sensation of breathing by using your diaphragm.* Later, much later, you'll be able to expand around the bottom of your ribs without pretending you're Santa Claus.

Don't worry if you feel silly moving your belly in and out. Once you get more advanced, your middle will simply widen. It will also contract more than before on the exhale. The result: when you do want to suck in your gut for a picture or do anything that involves your core muscles, you'll be able to do it better, for longer!

Does inhaling and having your middle expand feel completely counterintuitive? Surprise! You're probably a Paradoxical Breather (described in Chapter 3). You've been working against your body for years and have, in effect, been taking in a minuscule amount of air compared to what your body needs. This means that when your diaphragm is trying to flatten and help your lungs pull in more air, you're fighting against it. Sound exhausting? You're right, it is. Another good reason to fix this.

Put one hand on your belly and one on your chest, directly under your chin and between your collarbones. Spread your fingers so you can actually gauge movement. Change your breathing so that your top hand does not move at all and your belly expands, almost in an exaggerated way, on the inhale.

For contrast, do the opposite for a breath or two: have your bottom hand stay still, then gaze up and move your shoulders up on the inhale. Become fully aware of these two very different breaths.

All of this should make sense anatomically. When you breathe through the lower part of your body (expanding your middle, sides, and back), your diaphragm flattens out and pushes your bottom ribs out. On the exhale, your diaphragm curls up, narrowing your body as your lungs empty. Be patient with yourself. At first, it may seem as if there are too many pieces of information for you to juggle. Just keep repeating the belly breathing until it feels natural.

The exercises in this chapter will help you relearn how to breathe and will strengthen the right muscles, so that you'll feel as if you've actually done a workout at the gym.

WARMING UP YOUR DIAPHRAGM

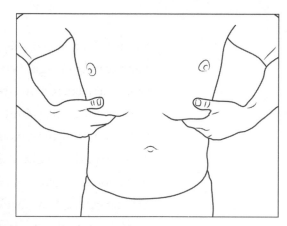

First, tap the bottom of your sternum with the tips of your fingers to bring your attention to that part of your body. Start walking your fingers slowly across the front of your bottom rib. Curve your fingers underneath that rib to bring awareness to the exact place where your diaphragm is connected. Imagine, in your mind's eye, how large this roundish muscle, which traverses your body from side to side, is. It also tilts back at your spine. Imagine how large your lungs are in the back: they spread to four fingers *above* your waistline!

LET'S GET STARTED

Now I want you to go through the four basic exercises that I teach in my class to strengthen all of the muscles involved in perfect respiration. *Note that all the breathing exercises should be done through the mouth for the first two weeks.*

> *FAQ: Do I have to breathe through my mouth?* Yes, while you're learning, breathing through your mouth will keep you paying attention to your breath, whereas breathing through your nose has a higher chance of your defaulting to your old dysfunctional way of breathing. Eventually, you'll definitely breathe regularly through your nose, since nose breathing has many benefits. We'll talk more about this later.

Rock and Roll

Sit on a chair or cross-legged on the floor. If you're sitting on a chair, don't lean back against the chair. If you're on the floor, make sure that you're seated on a blanket or pillow to give you a little height. On the inhale, expand your belly as you lean forward. If you're very thin, you may have to "push" your belly out to get the right posture in the beginning; if you're heavier around the middle, the sensation is about "releasing" your belly or putting it on your lap. On the exhale, lean back as if you were slumping on a couch: contract your belly, narrowing your waist, and exhale until you're completely empty.

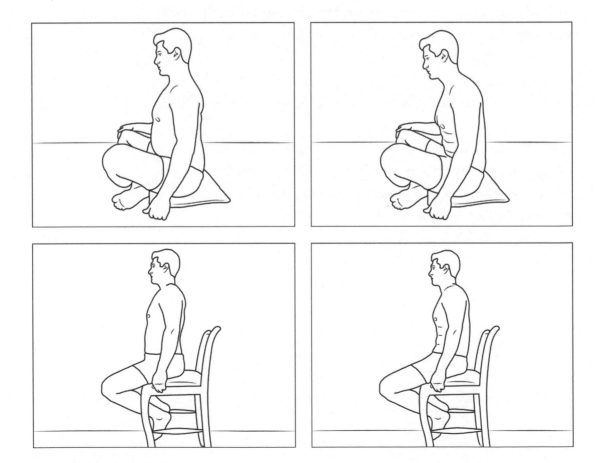

Right now, do 20 repetitions of this exercise.

Two things that should be kept in mind when doing Rock and Roll are *watching* and *listening* to your body. In front of a mirror, *watch* your middle expand and contract while doing these exercises. Remember that you're striving to be a Lower-body, Horizontal Breather, so your neck, shoulders, and upper chest don't move; they stay soft and relaxed. An inhale now means your middle expands, and on the exhale, like a sponge, squeezes in. At first, this may seem like two unrelated movements—breathing through your mouth and moving your middle—but soon they'll be synchronized and it will feel normal. Remind yourself that this less-than-sexy belly bulge movement will actually strengthen your core and middle and help you lose belly fat in the long run (plus, remember that we're doing the exaggerated version now while you learn; later, it will be much more subtle).

Listen to yourself so that you aren't holding your breath at the end of the inhale or the exhale. Keep in mind that every time you move your belly, you're actually "teaching" your diaphragm (which is right above your belly) to get activated when you breathe. Be ready for the sensation of "I've got it! Yes, this feels right!" to wax and wane. It *will* get to the point where it feels normal. Why? Because you used to breathe this way and your body wants to breathe this way again (that is to say, with the muscles it was given with which to inhale and exhale, rather than with your shoulders).

FAQ: Do you have to visibly rock forward and back? Yes, in the beginning. This movement keeps the breath low in your body, and lets you start doing other things (e.g., talking on the phone, reading) at the same time. The hip movement helps keep you in a Lower-body Breath. Later, the rocking will be very subtle—just a slight, undetectable hip pivot will be enough—but for now, really move back and forth, horizontally, so that the whole concept of Horizontal Breathing sinks in.

FAQ: Why don't you start by teaching me to breathe standing up first? Standing and breathing is actually more difficult. Plus, right now we sit much, much more than we stand, so learning to breathe while sitting is more useful. The standing breath is one that we're going to refine in steps, integrating the center of gravity, posture, and pelvic floor. You'll end up with perfect posture and perfect, healthy, beautiful breathing that will fuel your body and brain.

FAQ: Will these exercises actually strengthen my core? The abs exercises you do at the gym are usually ones related to your developing a six-pack. The muscles you use in exhaling are deeper core muscles. I've found that the athletes and gym enthusiasts with the most pronounced abdominals often don't have good exhale muscles, and even they are surprised when during Exhale Pulsations, an exercise we'll learn soon, they tire quickly.

FAQ: You said belly breathing "teaches" my diaphragm to move. When did it forget? When you were younger, your middle would expand and contract as your diaphragm pushed your ribs open and closed. When you started sucking in your gut and bracing your middle it got stuck, and yes, even temporarily paralyzed. Right now, we're "nudging it awake" until you'll be able to move it on your own.

Diaphragm Extensions

Lie down on your back. Place a large book (or a small stack of small books) on your abdomen, right on top of your belly button. Gaze toward the books—you should be able to see them at the very bottom of your field of vision. Take a belly breath with the goal of making the books rise, and on the exhale, watch them lower. You might find that your hips rotate slightly as you breathe, your lower back coming away from the floor slightly on the inhale. Bring awareness to and even exaggerate this movement. Go ahead and do 50 repetitions. Don't worry about your pace or counts right now; focus on getting used to the movement.

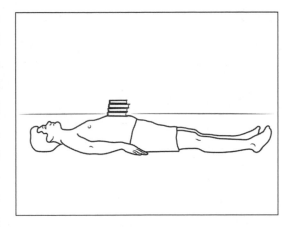

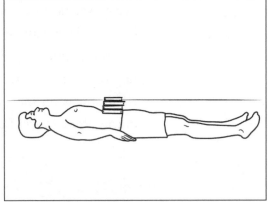

FAQ: What do I do if I find that I get distracted but am continuing to do the correct movement? This is good news. It means you're starting to acclimate to the new information and don't have to focus as much. *Bravo!*

As you get better at this exercise, you can graduate to heavier books or use a ten- or twelve-pound weight or kettlebell. When using a weight, hold it with one hand and move it to different parts of your middle: 2 inches above your belly button, to the right, then to the left. Keep holding the weight, but focus on pushing it away on the inhale and letting it drop toward you on the exhale. Really let this idea sink in: when you breathe, your middle moves, in both directions, always. Go ahead and do 20 repetitions in 5 different places on your middle.

FAQ: Isn't this going to make me gassy? While this is called a "belly breath," the fact is that air isn't going into your

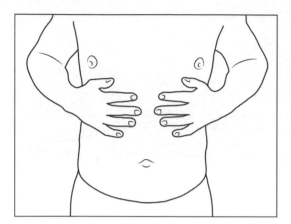

stomach at all. It's still going to your lungs, but now going to the bottom of your lungs, closer to your belly. The bottom of your lungs is where the densest, biggest lung tissue is, where the most exchange of oxygen happens.[26]

Now, let's look at the exhale part of this exercise. If you've really got it and are using a heavy weight, focus on letting the weight fall fully down into your body on the exhale, seeing how far you can narrow your waist. The heavier weight will help you achieve this. (This will make the "push up" that comes with the inhale more challenging, but the focus right now is on the exhale. Be careful not to hold your breath or brace). Remember: Let the weight push your belly button down toward your spine. Put the weight aside and see if, when you sit up, you can keep that hollowed out "C"-shape on the exhale. That's your goal.

"Exhale" doesn't mean "brace." If you exhale and find you're tensing, and your belly actually pops out, this is wrong. You want to get a scoop ("C"-shape) with your belly, bringing your belly button closer to your spine. More of this later, along with how you can add a Kegel (pelvic-floor contraction) along with the exhale.

FAQ: I've heard that my diaphragm contracts—is that on the inhale or exhale? Forget the word "contracts"; it confuses everyone. Right now, just think that on the inhale, your diaphragm flattens and pushes your ribs open, so that your middle should widen. And

---

26 For a brief overview of lungs and their function, with well-defined illustrations, go to http://patient.info/health/the-lungs-and-respiratory-tract.

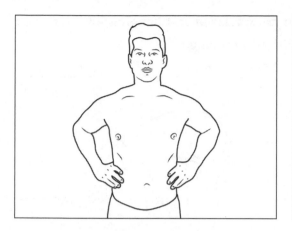 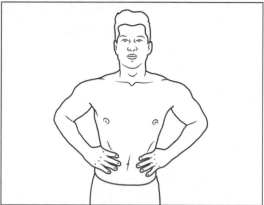

then the opposite, on the exhale. It curls closed and narrows your ribs.

FAQ: W*hat happens if I really can't "get" one of these exercises? Am I doomed to be a Vertical Breather forever?* Be gentle with yourself. Remind yourself you've had the bad habit of breathing vertically for years, maybe even decades, which means you've been breathing "wrong" thousands, yes, millions of times. Besides, this method is designed so that you have to find just one exercise that comes easily and work from there—you don't have to be able to "get" all of them initially. The bright side is that your body "wants" to breathe horizontally, and soon will have moments when it "remembers" doing it when you were young.

Cat and Cow

Get on your hands and knees to do this movement, often called "Cat and Cow" in yoga. Cat should resemble a Halloween-like hissing cat, with its back arched. Cow is the same, with an all-fours posture, but with your belly relaxed and hanging low, and your head positioned up as if you're mooing.

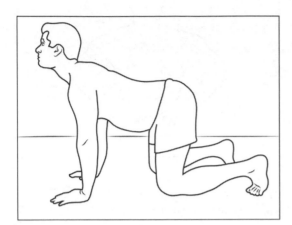 

Now, exhale audibly and round your back up into Cat. Then exhale more, simultaneously hollowing out your belly and blowing air out toward your belly button. Make sure your head is dropped completely, and you're stretching the back of your neck. Your tailbone should be tipped under. On the inhale, drop your body, relaxing your belly and letting it expand downward toward the floor. Let gravity help. Your tailbone should now be tipped out. Swivel your head upward as if you're looking toward the sky.

Do this 10 times right now, synchronizing the movement until it "flows" and you can easily rotate back and forth with each inhale and exhale.

Note of clarification: Your tailbone is your coccyx (it's where your tail would be if you had one); it should be "tipped out" when you inhale and "tipped under" when you exhale. See if any of the following helps you understand what "tipped under" on the exhale means:

• When you're sitting slumped on a sofa
• When you're in the Cat pose portion (exhale) of Cat and Cow

- When you're "flattening your butt," squeezing your glutes gently

If it still doesn't make sense to you, lie on the floor and press your lower back into the floor. Notice the rotation in your hips: you're tipping your tailbone under!

Your tailbone "tipped out" is the opposite:

- It's "bumping your butt back" ("selfie butt").
- It's the arch in your lower back when you're squatting at the gym.
- It's the curve in your lower back away from the chair seat on a Rock and Roll inhale.

DO THIS

When you're lying on the floor, create space between the floor and your lower back on the inhale. You should be able to slip your hand in between your lower back and the floor on the inhale.

FAQ: How do I "let go" of my belly? Make sure you're relaxing your hips, glutes, and thighs. Really focus on "softening" them. This will trigger your abs to relax so that you can expand better. (You might also try these exercises in a pool or hot tub: holding the side of the pool with your belly pointed downward, use gravity and the weight of the water to help you relax and expand your middle on the inhale.) Now, from Cat and Cow, sit back on your feet for

Challenge yourself to relax your belly more with each inhale and narrow harder with each exhale.

a second and do Rock and Roll seated upright. Notice how the movement is similar!

FAQ: What does "bumping your butt back" mean? When you tip your tailbone out on the inhale, make sure you're releasing your belly and expanding it at the same time. Often folks will "bump their butt back" and simultaneously suck in their gut—which is *not* what I want you to be doing. Inhale, pop your butt back, and let your belly go.

FAQ: When on the inhale I focus on really letting go of my stomach, down to the lowest muscles between my hip bones, it doesn't feel natural and I don't feel the two extremes. Am I doing something wrong? Check your Cat and Cow position: Your hands should be right under your shoulders; arms (especially elbows) and legs stay at perpendicular stable positions. You should not move back and forth; rather, you should move up and down. Let your head drop on the exhale—really relaxing and stretching the muscles on the back of your neck. On the inhale, stretch the front of your neck up, sipping air above and in front of you (air from the sky). It will take some concentration and practice until you can completely feel the two extremes—a total relaxing on the inhale and a squeeze and emptying out on the exhale. Not only is this a good stretch, but you get a lot of joint rotation that helps keep the joints in your hips and back lubricated and healthy. When you get more advanced, you might add Kegels[27] and Reverse Kegels[28] to this movement.

THE PERFECT STANDING BREATH

Change to a standing position and breathe the same way, but now with your arms at your sides. Make sure your shoulders do not engage in any way. Think of your arms as deadweights, heavy and immobile. This is best done standing sideways at a full-length mirror. Your neck, chest, and shoulders shouldn't move; only your belly and pelvis should be moving back and forth. As you let your belly expand forward, you should be arching your back a bit (your butt pops back slightly). On the exhale, contract your belly,

---

27 Kegels are pelvic-floor muscle exercises employed to strengthen the pubococcygeal muscle and other muscles of the pelvic diaphragm. The exercises were first described by Dr. Arnold Kegel in 1948. For an easy, step-by-step guide to how to perform the Kegel exercises, go to http://www.mayoclinic.org /healthy-lifestyle/womens-health/in-depth/kegel-exercises/art-20045283. I talk more about the pelvic floor in Chapter 10.

28 Reverse Kegels is a term coined by Isa Herrera, MSPT, CSCS. "Reverse Kegels are a lengthening and relaxation exercise for the PFMs [pelvic-floor muscles]. Once the PFMs have less tension, more flexibility, and less spasm, they can be strengthened using the typical Kegel exercise. Once the PFMs have had normal function restored, the patient will enjoy reduced pain, improved continence, enhanced sexual response, and improved daily function." For a full explanation of the role of pelvic exercise, go to her article, "Overcoming Pelvic Pain," at http://physical-therapy.advanceweb.com/Features/Articles/Overcoming -Pelvic-Pain.aspx.

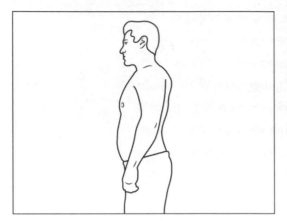 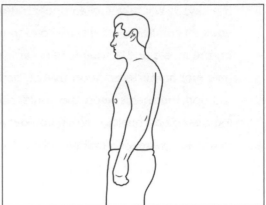

feel your lower abs tighten, and tuck in your butt (and you might give your glutes a slight squeeze to learn the movement).

Breathing this way is anatomically congruous; Vertical Breathing is not—you're going against the way your body and organs were built. A Lower-body Breath that expands on the inhale is a healthy breath. Tune in to how you're feeling; you'll find it feels right. You're not imagining it.

Breathing Sequence

Practice these four exercises in a sequence. This whole sequence should take from three to ten minutes.

- Do Rock and Roll 20 times (seated on the floor or on a chair).
- Roll over, lying on your back now, and do Diaphragm Extensions 20 times with a stack of books or with a weight.
- Roll over and push up onto all fours. Do Cat and Cow 20 times. Sit back on your feet momentarily (or come back onto a chair) and do 20 Rock and Roll Breaths again.
- Stand up and do the Perfect Standing Breath 20 times.

- On the inhale, you should be thinking two things: Lower-body Breath and expand. On the exhale think: Lower-body Breath and squeeze/contract. Remind yourself: "Inhale . . . expand. Exhale . . . squeeze."

Now that you know the mechanics, work on the quality. Most people have lazy inhales and even lazier exhales. Put some *oomph* into the two, and you'll expand your lung capacity by emptying out better as well as refilling with more air.

In addition, two subtle but very powerful benefits: an internal massage for your organs and a better flush of toxins from your body.

FAQ: I find that I "get it" for a little while, then I "lose it" and feel confused as to what to do. Pause, slowly cue yourself, and do it again. Do this watching yourself in the mirror, then alternate, closing your eyes and seeing if you can do it without a visual cue.

FAQ: This seems so long and drawn out—why don't you just instruct us to "take a belly breath"? We go through this sequence because just telling you to do a belly breath isn't going to change your habit of breathing vertically. In order to change something you've been doing for decades (you are a complex organism!), your brain has to understand how you got here, why you should change, and actually feel the results. It has to make sense intellectually and kinesthetically.

As often as you can, check your breathing throughout the day and make sure you are still breathing low. Even if you have to correct yourself each time, that is okay. Some people pause and bring their attention to their breath every hour on the hour, or before they look at texts. The more often you do it the better.

At some point, you'll check yourself and find you've stayed in a Lower-body Breath. *Hurray!* It's starting to sink in! Don't forget: your body wants to breathe this way (that's why you have a diaphragm), and you used to breathe this way when you were a child.

FAQ: I get a little dizzy doing this. Is that okay? Enjoy the light-headedness and buzz; there's no hangover! Think about how much more air is coming in and going out of your body. You're now using the biggest, densest part of your lungs and really exhaling well. A word of caution: in the beginning don't do these exercises while driving or running on a treadmill.

FAQ: What happens when I sleep—do I go back to my old bad patterns? Due to the fact that it's hard to breathe with an Upper-body Breath (UBB) when you're prone, most people go to a partial good Lower-body Breath when sleeping. Unfortunately, it doesn't make up for the long days of bad breathing and bracing (especially since most people aren't really sleeping as much as they should).

Do the Breathing Sequence twice a day *and* remind yourself as often as you can throughout the day.

FAQ: *Now that I'm used to it, my workout is only a couple minutes a day, but is more better?* Yes, ten minutes a day is the minimum. If you'd like to do two sets of ten minutes each, or add a couple of five-minute sessions throughout your day, go for it! As with anything, more practice means you'll get results faster and it will "sink" in better.

What do you achieve with the Perfect Breath?
Well, it:

1. activates your parasympathetic nervous system ("rest and digest")
2. lowers your blood pressure and heart rate
3. uses the lower, bigger, denser part of the lungs (i.e., your breathing is more efficient)
4. helps you avoid constipation, acid reflux, and irritable bowel syndrome
5. supports the health of your back and pelvic floor[29]
6. detoxifies your body by supporting the lymphatic system
7. balances acidity and lowers inflammation

Contrast the Perfect Breath with the dysfunctional Upper-body Breath (Vertical), which does none of these healthy things. In effect, a UBB creates pain in your shoulders and neck, raises your blood pressure and anxiety, and brings in much, much less oxygen.

INHALE MAXIMIZATIONS, AKA "AIR-PACKING"

Going through the steps below, you'll push air into parts of your lungs that have been passive. Free divers call this *"air-packing,"* but they do it more aggressively and with much more experience, so you'll only be doing a gentle version here.[30]

First, take a big Rock and Roll Breath. Continue "maximizing" your inhale by taking small sips of air. Do not exhale. You should feel your middle getting taut. Make sure you aren't bracing and

---

29 For more on the pelvic floor, see chapter 10.
30 An interesting and very readable article on air-packing appears on a University of Cambridge website, The Naked Scientists: http://www.thenakedscientists.com/HTML/interviews/interview/1000268/.

At the top of your breath (and remember, you aren't really filling *up*—you are filling *out*), relax your shoulders again and let the air feel as if it's settling into your body. Then soften your pelvis (meaning relax your glutes and thighs), and notice the feeling of being more grounded. This should only take two to three seconds.

Your diaphragm can move down about 4 inches (or 10 centimeters) and spread out up to 5!

During inspiration, an estimated two cups of "fresh" atmospheric air enters your body (less if you're a lazy breather!), but only the first cup and a half actually reaches the alveoli in your lungs. In fact, the remaining half-cup stays in your nose, larynx, trachea, and other airways without alveoli—basically, dead space.

tightening your body. Pause and consciously relax your middle, remembering that in order to take in more air, you have to soften and let your intercostals—the muscles between your ribs—stretch. (We'll actually do some stretches in the next section that are specifically for these muscles.)

Note where you feel tightness. Is it by your collarbones, armpits, in your back, where you might have an old injury? Gently stretch these places or use heat to heal and make them more flexible.

Now exhale, remembering that the exhale is an enthusiastic squeeze, not just a "letting go." Notice how long your exhale is now.

FAQ: Aren't my inhale and exhale just the same mechanism in reverse order? Not at all. Now that you are a Horizontal Breather, your inhale is governed primarily by the flattening out of your diaphragm, which pulls in air. Your exhale is more of a "recoil."

The next step is to address your lazy breathing. Start by taking a normal breath, that is, exactly like the one you took just before you started reading this.

Don't make this one "better" because now you're paying attention! Simply notice how you take in air until you meet some resistance in the inhale and stop; then your exhale is really just a letting go. Notice how passive this is. Imagine how much air you're taking in. The average is 12 ounces, or a cup and a half. If you had to measure the amount of air you inhale and exhale, what would it be? It might be even less, maybe a half-cup or even a few tablespoons—especially if you're sitting and concentrating in such a way that you completely disconnect from your body, such as while at a computer or driving. On your next exhale, put some attention into the emptying of air. Tighten your abs in an attempt to really squeeze out all the stale air.

Take five breaths, focusing intently on the exhale. Now bring your attention to your inhale. Notice how, even without trying, your inhale is automatically bigger. It's a more efficient breath because you've emptied out beforehand! Compare this breath to the one before in terms of efficacy. Remember that stale air stays in your lungs unless you consciously exhale it. Just keep training yourself to blow out every last little bit.

Then take it up a notch: On your next exhale, squeeze the last bit of air out with your core and ab muscles. And don't stop at a neutral (flat) stomach. Actually go one step further (to an inverted bowl shape); you might even push your fingers into your stomach and around your rib cage in order to become completely aware of the mechanics of this. Finally, scrunch up your face and pretend you are blowing out of a small straw. Don't worry if you cough a little.

So now you should understand that better breathing means better inhales and exhales. It's not just about getting more oxygen into your body; it's not that you

Asthma is a disorder related to poor exhales. If you or a loved one has asthma, make sure you see a doctor, but just as important, set up an exhale workout so that you can actually get better and reduce the need for an inhaler. This is the basis of the Russian breathing method called "Buteyko." The goal is to change your breathing from chronic hyperventilation (breathing too much) to slower, more balanced breathing with an emphasis on nasal breathing.

If you're a Paradoxical (or Reverse) Breather, the exhale is really your friend. Make it a rule always to start your breathing with an exhale. It will remind you to take a Lower-body Breath and you'll go on to a horizontal inhale, rather than having to correct yourself from an Upper-body Breath over and over. Try it and see.

want a bigger inhale. It's about having a balance of both. Having an imbalance of oxygen and carbon dioxide can create serious problems related to inflammation and acidity. But without delving into the chemistry, simply know that you need to pay attention to both.

As you practice these exercises, take comfort in the thought that although you should focus on your belly, I don't expect you to continue pushing out your abdomen with every single inhale forever. This is just a way to start reconditioning your body so it will do what it should be doing naturally; eventually, this won't look or feel silly. Focus on the expansion and contraction of your middle without your shoulders moving. Both of these movements work your core, so that better breathing will lead naturally to stronger ab and core muscles.

TOXINS AND YOUR INTERNAL DRAINAGE SYSTEM

You've heard a lot lately about toxins and how "eating clean," drinking more water, and having better bowel movements help get them out of your system, but the most important way we get rid of toxins is by breathing—both through the air we breathe out *and* through the movement of lymph in the body, which is aided by good whole-body breathing. The lymphatic system is a little-talked-about sewer system for your body, taking debris and toxins your cells excrete into your circulatory system through two ducts at the base of your neck. Now, your lymph system doesn't have a built-in pump; rather it relies on the circulation stimulated by breathing to move all that waste fluid. If you don't breathe well, you're going to have a sluggish "drainage" system that doesn't detoxify you properly.

A sluggish lymphatic system can lead to health concerns over time, including weight gain, muscle loss, high blood pressure, fatigue, and inflammation. But the great news is: improve your breathing and detoxify better! The expansion and contraction of the diaphragm actually stimulates your lymphatic system and massages your internal organs, helping the body rid itself of toxins and leaving more room in the cells for an optimal exchange of oxygen. As you change to being a Horizontal Breather, you aren't imagining things—you feel better.

> *FAQ: When I exhale like this, does it count as an abs workout?* Absolutely. It's not just ab muscles that give you a six-pack; in effect, there are more important ones deeper inside that have to do with core and pelvic stability.

> *FAQ: I feel as if I still have air stuck inside of me—any other suggestions?* Try a Lion's Breath pose from yoga—stick your tongue way out toward your chin on the exhale. Yes, it feels silly but it's very effective. Notice how much air was left over from your normal lazy exhale as compared to your more attentive one. Think of all the wasted space that you could fill with clean air. *Roar!*

> *FAQ: Exhaling and contracting my stomach doesn't seem natural—is that okay?* Yes, it is, because in order to relearn this, cough and see which way your belly goes. I bet you it tightens, right? Keep this in mind as you retrain your body. Be patient.

BEFORE MOVING ON TO THE NEXT
EXERCISE, REFINE YOUR MOVES

When you're on your back, hold a 6-, 8-, or 10-pound weight on your stomach (or, if you feel as if you can handle it, use a small kettle-bell), and see how far you can let it fall into your stomach as you exhale. You might want to pick a heavier weight; this is not about raising it, but about seeing how close you can get your belly to your spine, narrowing your middle. *Be careful not to bounce the weight.* Sit up, seeing how close you can come to keeping that "bowl" shape while sitting and exhaling. After you've worked on these expiration muscles for a while, you'll be able to maintain that concave bowl shape in your middle. When you're doing Exhale Maximizations, try to mimic the amount of "inward" curve you can get with the weight. You can expect this to be hard. While you're used to bracing your middle, the "pull inward" is a different set of muscles.

To make Rock and Roll part of my daily routine, I set my phone alarm to vibrate every hour on the hour during the day. That way, no matter where I am, as soon as I hear or feel the vibration, I don't even pause: I just lean back slightly and exhale, then lean forward and inhale. No one even notices I'm doing it. The slight rock back and forth means I can even go on to do other things, as long as I'm breathing "with my hips" and not my shoulders. —Josephine, age 50

FACTOID: The lungs can hold about 6 quarts in males, 4.4 quarts in females; the residual volume (what usually remains in the lungs) is about a quart.

Sitting and breathing like this wasn't working easily, so it was a relief to lie on my back and try it. After practicing like this, I was able to sit up and try Rock and Roll again—and it was easier. Keeping my eyes open and really thinking about how the pile of books should rise if I was inflating underneath them made so much sense it was almost silly. It helps to have a sense of humor when you realize you've been breathing wrong for so long. —Monty, age 41

I couldn't believe I'd been doing yoga for so long and had the breathing with Cat and Cow backward. But fixing it made sense first in my head, so I was able to correct myself. Of course, during Cow I should be inhaling; why it was the same move as seated Rock and Roll—just in another position! —Satchi, age 33

Letting go of my belly was hard. Even when I thought I had totally let go, I found I could relax a little more. Seeing my belly from the side view was humbling, but then I got to exhale and squeeze it— and feeling how strong I'd be able to make it made me feel better. After two weeks, even though I was still chunky, I could see a line starting to form where my abs were working. I'd never seen any lines of any sort on my belly! —Buddy, age 29

I did belly breathing on my side and in the bathtub. I found that if I added positions of my own, it felt completely different, as if I was "getting it" even better. —Nisse, age 26

I work as a customer service rep on the phone, which means I have plenty of time to do my breathing exercises. And it's true: if I keep doing a slight Rock and Roll I can listen, write, and work on the computer and almost not think about it. —Cooper, 46

I've always felt kind of numb around my middle. Moving my breathing down there was weirdly eye-opening. All of a sudden, it just wasn't my middle and hips—that part of my body got more sensation and became more important. And it made sense. The biggest part of my lungs is above my belly button! And my diaphragm goes all the way around my body! It felt good to understand my own anatomy in a way I never had before. I moved the weight around my middle and inhaled, pushing it away. The very practical, tactile nature really helped get the idea ingrained in my head. —Miranda, age 51 ✑

I work at a lighting store, so I got creative and acquired two 8-pound sandbags that are used to hold down supplies. I put them on my shoulders, which made Vertical Breathing hard and made me go back to a Horizontal style. Sure, I had to change to clothes that would let me breathe horizontally, but that was in fact a relief. No more tight waists. I kept reminding myself that breathing this way would actually make my core and abs stronger in the long run. And I also kept in mind that when I'd look down and see my belly (and say ugh!), this was intro breath 101—eventually I'd be able to do a 360-degree Lower-body Breath. —Gabriella, 34 ✑

5

STRETCH AND WARM UP

When you pack your knapsack or suitcase most efficiently, you use up every little nook and cranny, shifting things around to maximize space. This is what you're going to do with your lungs, which may result in your ability to access fuller lung capacity. The truth is that, even if you have Aquaman-size lungs, it matters little if your thoracic cavity (rib cage) and the muscular encasement that holds your lungs are rigid.

These muscles (see figure 3a), which include the ones between each and every rib, help you inhale and exhale to your full potential. This chapter and the next will help you utilize the maximum capacity of your lungs and ensure that the encasement

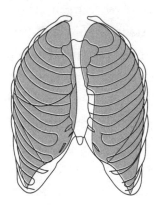
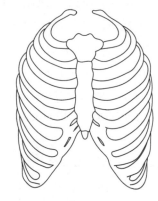

Figure 3a   Figure 3b

Just the attention that you are paying to your breathing, just the awareness you are bringing to it a few times a day, even sporadically, means you have started to change—to get better. You are taking in more air than yesterday, even if all you are doing is bringing attention to your breath from time to time.

(see figure 3b) of your lungs is as flexible as possible in order to help, not hinder, your breathing.

The exercises in this chapter will set you on your path to better health and performance by helping you rethink your own respiration. And it's as simple as transforming the most basic components of a breath: your inhalations and exhalations.

EXHALE MAXIMIZATIONS

The exhale is the underdog—it's really much more important than it gets credit for. It may seem counterintuitive, because when you think about breathing, your mind automatically goes to your inhale. In fact, most people barely exhale at all, let alone fully; yet *mediocre exhalations are a major contributor to poor breathing and hence have negative repercussions on your overall health.*

Between each breath, a small amount of carbon dioxide stays in your lungs, just settling there and getting stale (and if you are a really lazy exhaler, it may be even more). The result is that these organs can't expand to their full capacity with fresh air on your next inhalation. In other words, your starting inhalations *have* to be less than optimal when you haven't exhaled well. (Often the result is that you speed up the rate of your breathing in an effort to compensate, which ripples outward to cause an imbalance of pretty much everything in your body and nervous system.)

With the following exercises, I'm going to show you how to squeeze out as much of that stale air as possible on your exhales, so there will be plenty of room in your lungs for new, oxygen-rich air. Let's work on making that better.

1. On your next exhale, put some attention into the emptying of air. Does working your abs at the same time count as multitasking? Absolutely. It's not just the abdominal muscles that give you a six-pack; in effect, there are more important ones, deeper inside, that have to do with core and pelvic stability.

2. Take it up a notch: On your next exhale, squeeze the last bit of air out with your core and ab muscles. And don't stop at a neutral (flat) stomach. Actually go one step further (to a bowl shape); you might even push your fingers into your stomach and around your rib cage to become completely aware of the mechanics of this. (Supine or lying on your back or leaning over works best when you are starting out because of gravity.) Finally, scrunch up your face and pretend you are blowing out of a small straw. Don't worry if you cough a little. Notice how much air was left over from your normal lazy exhale, as compared to your more attentive one. Think of all the wasted space that you could fill with clean air.

3. Take five normal breaths, focusing intently on the exhale. On the next five breaths, concentrate on taking a really big inhale. Notice how your inhale is automatically a bigger, more efficient breath because you have emptied out beforehand. Compare this breath to the one before in terms of efficacy. Remember that stale air stays in your lungs unless you consciously exhale it. Just keep training yourself to blow out every last little bit.

Do This

Barely exhale, then go to your inhale. Continue for another five or six breaths like this, having your exhale be only a fraction of your inhale. Notice how it is possible to continue breathing in this way. Become aware that, given injuries, posture, and bad habits, it would be easy to fall into the trap of always breathing this way (on a much more subtle level, of course). Now think about the math; think about breathing this way for months, for years. Despite feeling as if you are taking a deep breath, your inhale is very shallow, and the actual exchange of oxygen and carbon dioxide is completely out of balance.

INHALE MAXIMIZATIONS AND STRETCHES

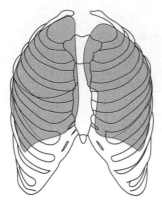

The next stage in maximizing your inhalations is to consider the flexibility of your thoracic cavity. If you sit at a desk at work or spend several hours a day in a car, then your thoracic cavity is probably pretty darn rigid—the size of your lungs doesn't matter. Making the intercostal muscles (between your ribs, in your sides and back—see figure 3c) more flexible means they will expand more, allowing you to take a bigger breath.

Figure 3c

Intercostal Stretch

Sitting up straight, drape one arm over your head so that the bicep is covering your ear. Visualizing the little muscles in between each rib on your side, stretch in the opposite direction, keeping your elbow straight up. Watch yourself in the mirror and make sure the majority of the stretch is not coming at your armpit. You might hold your side with your opposite hand just to give yourself some tactical awareness of where you want to be stretching. Do not hold your breath. *Inhale* during the stretch and *exhale* when you relax a bit or straighten up. Then reverse sides.

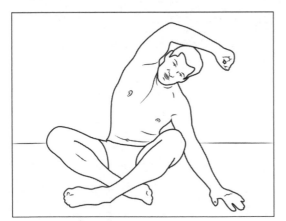

Think of the intercostal stretch as a *side* belly breath. Your diaphragm can expand on the sides; this stretch is helping to activate that as well.

FAQ: Shouldn't I be exhaling as I stretch, like I do with other stretches? No. You want to fill the space with air and then stretch, so that the muscles *inside* have to give a little more. It does feel counterintuitive in the beginning, but if you keep the image of these between-the-rib muscles in your mind's eye, it will make sense to you.

FAQ: Will I be breathing more into one lung when I do this? Yes, and the reason is that your breathing might feel slightly restricted, as compared to a "front" belly breath.

The intercostal stretch can be done standing next to the wall as well, with one palm on the wall.

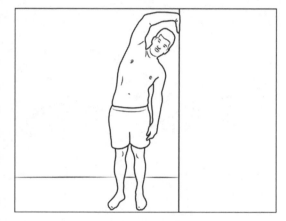

Inhale and "open" your side. Move your feet closer to or farther from the wall to find places at your side that feel tighter. The arm closest to the wall should stretch down toward your knee as you feel the stretch in your rib cage.

Now lie down on your side with one arm resting along the length of your body and do this exercise. Does it feel as if you're pushing that arm up on the inhale? Even if it's subtle, if this resonates with you, it means you're really starting to breathe through the middle of your body, where the densest part of your lungs are, with your diaphragm, the way you're meant to. *Bravo!*

After you have done this exercise, take a deep breath, with awareness on the in-

If you have a high tolerance for pain, don't do these exercises to the top of your pain threshold. Remember that these little muscles have been pretty still for a long time, so be gentle.

side of your arms between your armpits and elbows. The parts that touch your sides. Notice how you can feel your sides expand. "Play" with this new sensation by doing the breathing exercises in different positions.

Next Step

Then, do the Child's Pose to bring awareness to your back. Remember, your chin should almost fit between your knees; keep 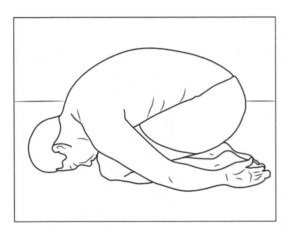 your arms back with your shoulders "melting" down as you relax with each breath. If you have difficulty pointing your toes back, dropping your head low enough to get to the floor, or trouble with your lower back, try a supported Child's Pose: put a rounded pillow or bolster vertically from your tummy to your head, or between your calves and butt to lessen the pressure if you are still too stiff or need the extra support. Inhale and puff up your back, exhale and flatten your body.

V-back Opener

Round your back, extending your arms in front of you. Inhale. Clasp your hands together, palms facing out. Drop your head. Focus on increasing the gap between your hands and your chest, feeling your shoulders stretch across your back.

Become aware of Lateral Breathing—the expansion of your thoracic cavity from side to side that you will feel when you cross your arms in front of you, putting your hands on your sides or your hands in opposite armpits, as if keeping them warm—notice the

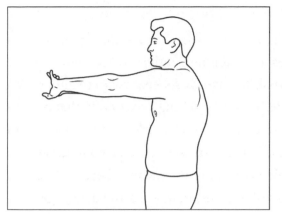 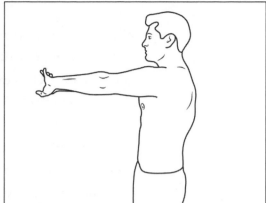

expansion of your back and sides when you breathe, this exercise
will change subtly.

*FAQ: I feel like my ribs are moving a bit more now when I
breathe. Is that okay?* Yes. You'll notice that subtly, you are
moving from a belly breath to a real middle-of-your-body
breath. This is good; it's the goal. Your intercostals are very
important; in fact, the beginner belly breath is really just
the starting point for your feeling your entire middle moving without engaging your shoulders. External intercostals
pull your ribs open for the inhale; internal intercostals close
for the exhale.

*FAQ: You talk about activating the diaphragm; when did it
deactivate?* It started when you started bracing your body,
either as an emotional response or when sucking in your gut
because you thought it was good for you. Little by little,
your diaphragm got replaced by your neck and shoulder
muscles, which would pull you up to breathe. Not to worry,
though, because your understanding, stretching, and practicing the exercises now will get it back in gear, no matter
how old you are.

Refining Your Moves

While your body is neutral and relaxed, try sliding your fingers slightly under your ribs and tugging gently, pulling your ribs out (horizontally). Then exhale and lightly squeeze them together with the palms of your hands. This is "teaching" your body that breathing means there is movement in your whole body, especially in your middle, where the biggest, densest part of your lungs are. Eventually, you'll develop control of the muscles here and be able to do this on your own, using your intercostals and diaphragm.

FAQ: I feel like I am pushing my belly out but my diaphragm isn't expanding, is this possible? It's unusual but *yes*. It probably means you're tensing up too much in an attempt to get a bigger belly. Don't push your belly out so hard; rather, think of your entire middle softening and expanding. You might even put a measuring tape slightly above your belly, right at your diaphragm (exactly where you measured Vital Lung Capacity) and use it as a tactile cue that points to the place where you should really be expanding. All these muscles and your diaphragm inside have been underutilized. You have to become aware of them and stretch and strengthen them. The good news is you'll have small "aha!" moments along the way, where all of a sudden you feel as if you get it.

FAQ: My back is sore when I breathe, which has never happened before. Is that normal? It's normal. Think about it—your diaphragm goes all around your body, including your back. When you exhale, all your middle-body mus-

The belly breath really is just the beginner breath that helps break down the habit of keeping the middle of your body braced. It gets you physically used to the idea that there's movement from your armpits to your pelvis when you breathe.

cles contract a bit, even your back muscles. Though the movement isn't a big one, you're moving muscles you haven't used like this in decades.

FAQ: Every once in a while, I get a stitch when doing the breathing exercises—should I worry? No; it sounds as if you have a cramp in a muscle—a cramp you'd get in your calf or side when you run. Try relaxing your body and giving it a moment for the stitch to subside.

FAQ: When I exhale, am I trying to narrow my whole body, sides, and back, too, or just the abs in the front? Whereas the beginner exhale is only focusing on your abs, once this all becomes more natural, you can think about your whole body—from your armpits to your pelvis—contracting, much like a sponge.

FAQ: When I do the intercostal stretch exercise, I "lose" the belly breath. Is that okay? As long as you're not using your shoulders to inhale, that's fine. This is really about stretching these muscles so that when you're upright, you're taking a better breath. Think about it as a side belly breath. You actually have a lot of lung space on your side, so this may feel even more natural than a belly breath. Remember that the long-term goal is to be breathing all the way around your body in Lower-body Breaths, without using your shoulders.

FAQ: So if I'm not making a belly breath, am I still breathing with my diaphragm? Yes, if you're breathing with a Lower-body Breath, not using your shoulders and feeling yourself expand on the inhale and contract/squeeze on the exhale, you're starting to use your diaphragm from all sides. Re-member, it's a lot like an umbrella in your body that pushes your ribs open (wider) when you inhale, and then on the exhale, closes and encourages your body to contract and squeeze out.

Twists and Diaphragm Activation

Spinal twists are my favorite stretches—they're the king of all stretches and they help keep your body and posture young and healthy. I'm going to show you how to do them on the ground, sitting, and stand-ing. If you do one stretch during the day, make it your favorite one.

Twists can provide a great number of benefits to your spine, hips, and digestive system. There should be *no* pain when they're per-formed.

Seated Spinal Twist

1. Sit on a folded blanket, legs straight out in front of you.
2. Draw your knees up close to your chest with both feet on the floor.
3. Drop your right leg down and then lift your left leg and place it over your right leg, knee toward the ceiling, left ankle

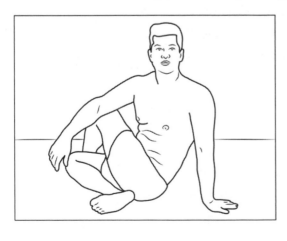

by the right knee. Repeat on the other side.
4. Draw your right leg toward the body.
5. Inhale a Lower-Body breath, feeling your belly expand, and then, on an ex-hale, bring your left elbow to the outside of your right knee as you twist toward your right.
6. Hold the pose for 5 to 10 seconds. Re-peat on the other side.

An easier variation is keeping one leg straight as pictured on the right.

Reclined Spinal Twist

1. Lie on your back, with your knees bent and your feet flat on the floor. You can rest your head on a pillow or blanket for extra neck support. Let your arms rest at your sides.

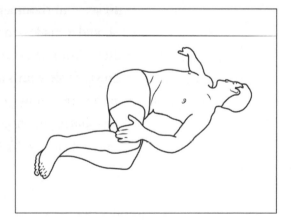

2. On an exhalation, draw both knees to your chest and clasp your hands around them.

3. Extend your left leg along the floor, keeping your right knee drawn to your chest. Extend your right arm out along the floor at shoulder height.

4. Shift your hips slightly to the right. Then, place your left hand on the outside of your right knee. Exhaling, drop your right knee over the left side of your body. Keep your left hand resting gently on your right knee. Turn your head to the right.

Try Simple Adjustments to Make Reclined Spinal Twist Relaxing:

• Rest your top knee and leg on a bolster or firm pillow.
• Place a folded blanket between your legs.

Variation

1. Cross your right knee over your left knee (crossing knee-to-knee). If you have the flexibility, also wrap your right foot around your left calf, coming into the Eagle Legs pose.

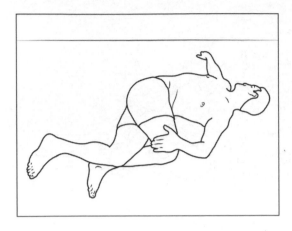

2. Shift your hips slightly to the right and drop your knees to the left.

3. Come back to center, then repeat on the opposite side.

Practicing Reclined Spinal Twist can be calming and comforting. Keep the following information in mind when practicing this pose:

- Bring your top knee over only as much as comfort will allow. If needed, rest your top knee on a bolster or pillow to decrease the range of motion.
- Keep your breath smooth; do not hold your breath.
- Rest the opposite hand on your top knee to gently add more weight.
- Relax your shoulders away from your ears. Try to keep both shoulder blades on the floor.
- Relax your abdominal muscles.
- Never force your knee to the floor. Be gentle with yourself!
- Be aware of how your back feels during the pose. If you feel any sharp, pinching, or jabbing pain, stop the pose and come out of it slowly. Never force the twist if you're in pain.

Seated Twist

Sit sideways on a chair. Twist to the left so your torso is facing the chair back and grasp it with your hands. If your neck will permit it, complete the full spinal twist by looking over your left shoulder. Swing around to the right and repeat. Remember: twist at the waistline; resist using the chair's back to wrench your body around further into the twist.

Standing Twist

Place a chair next to a wall. Bend the leg closest to the wall and place it on the chair. This time, when you twist, place your hands on the wall to hold yourself in a deeper position—but walk them back toward center if your back starts to protest. Repeat on the opposite side.

Benefits of Spinal Twists

1. Therapeutic for carpal tunnel syndrome[31]
2. Relieve thoracic or mid-back spinal tension
3. Strengthen your abdominal oblique muscles
4. Stretch your hip rotators and hips
5. Lengthen, relax, and realign the spine
6. Massage your abdominal organs and stimulate digestion
7. Benefit the soft tissues that surround the spine
8. Enhance the health of the discs and facet joints between the vertebrae

TWISTS *AND* BREATH

Once you've mastered these twists, integrate the breath. There are several reasons:

1. Usually, when put in a restrictive position, you'll go up to an Upper-body Breath. Now you want to teach your body that, no

---

31 Marian S. Garfinkel et al., "Yoga-based Intervention for Carpal Tunnel Syndrome: A Randomized Trial," *Journal of the American Medical Association* 280, no. 18 (1998): 1601–03.

matter what, your breathing stays low. Yes, it's tough to inhale and expand your middle and exhale and contract when pretzeled up and stretching. Do it anyway.

2. As your body is twisting and stretching, so are your lungs and organs. Breathing low while in a stretch helps to massage your organs at a different angle as well as to detoxify (think of wringing out a wet washcloth).

3. Depending on which side you're stretching, one lung is working harder than the other. This automatically will help expand your lung capacity to sections of your lungs you may not use much, or at all.

After having done these warm-up exercises and stretches, your Vital Lung Capacity will already have improved. This can be measured with a fabric measuring tape pre- and post-exercise.[32] What was your original inhale number? What was your original exhale number? Right now, see if you've expanded at least ¼ inch for each, getting a bigger inhale and a smaller, more efficient exhale. Make sure you're not using your shoulders anymore. Take the measurement several times, focusing on making that number bigger on the inhale and smaller on the exhale. Nudge and prompt yourself in either direction, sipping in air, "letting it settle," seeing if straightening up or relaxing helps the air go down, then push the measuring tape to a slightly bigger number on the inhale.

Initially, the idea of doing the breathing throughout the day was overwhelming. So I started doing a few minutes in the morning, before lunch, before dinner, and in bed at night. That worked for me. I actually looked forward to these "pauses" that made me slow down

---

32 If you like math and measurements, you might want to check out http://www.biologycorner.com/worksheets/lungcapacity.html.

and focus on me. Each time, I did have to switch over to the Horizontal Breath, but each time, it was easier and seemed more "natural." I really maximized my inhale and exhale for these breaths—focusing on taking a few really big expansive breaths, and really squeezing all the way out on the exhale. Plus, I figured if each Lower-body Breath was worth six of the Vertical ones I was taking during the rest of the day, I was still doing myself a great service by taking almost a hundred bigger breaths in total and pushing the amount of oxygen I was giving my body and brain up a huge percent. —Ted, age 37

Jason's Story

A friend who was concerned about his mental health had dragged Jason to the class. A massive man who had played football in college, Jason worked in senior management in construction. He was obviously reticent and skeptical, needling me with mild sarcasm about a "breathing class." "I don't have time to breathe," was his first announcement. His wife had died six months earlier, and he'd been left with their two children and a stressful job. As he relaxed, he finally was able to admit that he had a feeling of tightness in his chest, and that it felt hard to take a deep breath. He often felt "fuzzy" and off center. Once he was able to open up a bit more, he confided that he was scared of crying in public. Jason reported a sense of relief when breathing horizontally. He relaxed as he found himself agreeing on the basic tenets and straightforward explanations presented in class.

RETESTING YOUR VLC

1. While the VLC can give you concrete numbers, you want to "reach for" a more expansive inhale (bigger number) and a smaller exhale (smaller number). The main idea, then, is that you want your inhale to be wider and your exhale to be narrower. The more change you see between these two numbers, the better. Measuring yourself from time to time to see your progress will help you really integrate the idea that your middle moves when you breathe. Working on the flexibility of your rib cage and back will help this number get better as well.

2. As you work on making your middle more mobile, you're going to focus on your shoulders staying relaxed. If they move, it should be minimal. The goal is a Lower-body Breath—a high VLC, without your shoulder muscles being the main ones involved.

3. Keep the measuring tape loose and put serious effort into having your belly "meet" it. If you're advanced, you might go back and forth, seeing if you can add expansion from the sides and back. Air-pack and relax your middle, observing if that helps the expansion.

4. On the exhale, use the tape to squeeze you, to help your body "understand" that the exhale is almost a "wringing out" of air, where all the muscles from your armpits to your pelvis flatten out and narrow.

   While this is obviously an exaggerated breath, as when learning anything new that's mechanical, doing the exaggerated version in the beginning helps the learning process.

6

THE WORKOUT

You're not getting on the treadmill and you don't have to pick out weights, but this is an internal workout where you'll break a sweat and burn some calories.

EXHALE PULSATIONS—CANDLE BLOWS

Exhale Pulsations are short, sharp exhales that work the muscles involved with exhalation. You might think of them as a pumping action. With this exercise, your abs move from neutral to concave (or at least to a concave feeling).

Your belly scoops in—even if you have fat around your middle that doesn't naturally "go in." It should feel as if the muscles are pulling your belly button deeper into your body than ever before. Pretend you're blowing out a row of candles on a big cake that's across the table. When you exhale through your mouth, let the air hit *the back of your teeth* in order to make noise on the exhale.

There are three important things to remember when doing Exhale Pulsations:

1. Don't move your back. (Exhale Pulsations don't have the same back-and-forth movement as Rock and Roll.)

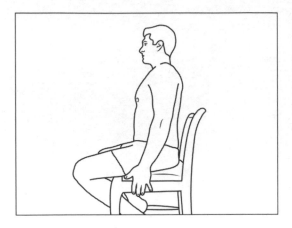 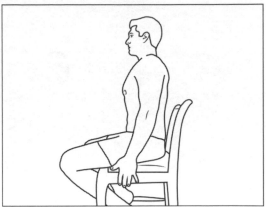

2. Even though you do inhale a bit, the focus is on blowing out air; this is an *exhale* exercise.

3. Make sure both the abs movement and the exhale are in synch! Although you may want to go for bigger numbers, resist the temptation and focus on the quality. The inward scoop motion of your belly should happen at exactly the same time as you "blow out the candles."

If you have high blood pressure, *be gentle!* Fast reps can raise your blood pressure, so stay at a slower pace—at under sixty reps a minute. Whereas research from the Patanjali Institute in India shows that slower Exhale Pulsations are safe for people with blood pressure issues, err on the side of caution—but don't skip this exercise altogether. The good news is that all the exercises in this book will play an important part in *lowering* your blood pressure, as early as the first week you start practicing.

FAQ: I cough and yawn when I do these exercises. Is this normal? Yes, and it's actually good. It means you're pushing yourself and shaking your body out of a normal sedentary breathing state.

FAQ: This is so hard, how come? What muscles am I using, exactly? To exhale, you use your inner intercostals (the muscles on the very inside of your ribs), your obliques (on your sides), your abs, your inner core/pelvic-floor, and even your back muscles. You might feel a little sore after doing exhales using your lower body because, as with any exercise you've never done before, you lack practice.

Exhale Pulsations are similar to Breath of Fire in yoga, a breath that's supposed to purge and clear out your system. According to yoga philosophy, a round of this breath will help you feel less irritable and angry. Later, when we talk about patterned breathing, we can join this to a breath count and you can see how it really does work, taking you from annoyed to relaxed in a few seconds. It's also similar to the "stick" or "ttsss" sound that boxers make when they jab, synchronizing the punches and breathing and hence making the blows more precise and powerful.

> *FAQ: How was I exhaling before?* Before, you were using your shoulders to exhale: letting them fall and relaxing your belly—a very, very ineffective way to exhale.

Mix it up: Try to do the exercise fast without losing the synchronicity of the abs squeeze and the exhale: slow down the "pulse," holding the squeeze a bit longer, and making the exhale audible and powerful. If you've never done this before, it'll help if you put one finger up at arm's length in order to feel the exhale. This is an ab exercise that targets deeper core muscles and will enable you to exhale more effectively. Stronger exhale muscles and more conscious exhaling are very important because they create more space in your lungs for fresh air, thereby making your inhale more effective. When you exhale passively, you leave stale air in your lungs. By strengthening your exhale muscles, you will exhale better unconsciously.

More advanced: Blow harder between ten and twenty times,

aiming for a place farther off in the distance. Make the exhale really audible. Exhale harder, with the goal of seeing a concave scoop in your middle when you stand sideways looking at yourself in a mirror. Blow out harder and squeeze your middle, narrowing it, harder. Slow down, so that the compression feels very intense and you feel a burn sooner. Try pulling your belly button as close to your spine as you can. Switch to your nose—this automatically makes the inhale and exhale harder, since your nostrils are smaller than your mouth.

FAQ: On the exhale, I feel as if I tighten, even push my belly out. This is wrong, right? Yes, it's wrong, this is not the right way to do it. You want your belly muscles to be narrowing and creating a "C"-scoop. Try to do this without the breath in order to see how you're using completely different muscles. Slow down! Even if you're on the heavier side and don't get that sucked-in shape, the feeling and muscles used are the same.

DETERMINE YOUR BASELINE

Count how many Exhale Pulsations you can do in a row. *Be careful: it's easy to continue to blow and not contract your stomach.* Keep an eye out that you aren't cheating! The best way to do this is to have someone watch you or to watch yourself. (It's better to do five, ten, or fifteen perfect ones than fifty casual or sloppy ones.) Note the number; write it down.

FAQ: How do I know when I've gotten to my max? You're at your max when you can't do any more pulsations with the same range of movement and enthusiasm as the first ones. If you went from a pulsation to a flutter, you're done.

And keep in mind:

Exhale Pulsations are easy to do throughout the day, since they're inconspicuous. You don't have to break your record each time; just do half or a quarter of your max for exercise.

Remember to stick to breathing through your mouth. Later, you might switch to your nose.

When you go to the gym and want to know how much weight to use or how to increase the amount of reps, you go by the point at which you "max out"—where your muscle or body part gets so fatigued that you have to stop. It's the same thing with Exhale Pulsations: Do them until you can't do any more. This will give you a baseline to work from.

FAQ: *I find doing Exhale Pulsations through my mouth pretty easy. How do I do them through my nose?* Pretending a bug landed near or up your nostril and you're trying to blow it out is a cue that works for me.

Troubleshooting

- Make sure that each "pulsation" is as strong as the next. When you see that you're giving a weaker or smaller squeeze than your first ones, it means you have fatigued that muscle—and that's your max. Have someone else give you feedback. Number thirty-five may feel right to you but look much weaker to an outside viewer. Once the quality starts suffering, you've reached your max.

- Make sure you're really giving one squeeze for each blow. Sometimes you can get carried away with the rhythm and quick pace, and lose synchronicity between the two. When your belly gets tired, it might squeeze every second blow, rather than every one. If that happens, you're done! Note your number.

- Don't judge. Whatever number you get to, having done the pulsations accurately, is just fine. This is a number you're starting at. It may be ten, it may be one hundred. You see people at the gym swinging weights wildly, not really getting the complete movement they want (and so essentially "cheating"). Be firm with yourself so that you get an accurate number. The important thing is that this is your baseline, and it's going to get better with practice, and soon.

HOW TO ADD EXHALE PULSATIONS TO YOUR WORKOUT

1. Exhale Pulsations are a "satisfying" exercise. The targeted muscles respond quickly to exercise. Other muscles take a long time

EXHALE PULSATIONS
MAX: 40
HOMEWORK: 20, 8x a day
GOAL: Improve max to 60 by next week

to get stronger, and it can be frustrating. Once you pay a little attention to these exercises, you'll see the number rise—every week!

2. Consider finding a partner. Doing the exercises side by side with someone else can help push you beyond what you might do on your own. Every two weeks, check your max again: Did you go up ten or twenty? *Bravo!* Your exhale muscles are getting stronger.

3. If you get dizzy while doing Exhale Pulsations, don't worry about it. Just don't do these exercises while standing, running, or driving. A little light-headedness is expected; however, if you experience anything worse, either pause and rest or slow down. But if you're able to do one hundred Exhale Pulsations and need a harder exercise, or just want to see what's coming up once you get to the hundreds, this next exercise will give you an idea.

ADVANCED EXHALE PULSATIONS—IN "TABLETOP" POSITION

Get down on all fours. Pretend you're a table, staying completely still—except for your belly. (Gravity is your friend in this position.) Let your belly drop. It's best to watch yourself in a mirror; you probably don't let your belly drop completely. Relax your body, especially your hips—but be careful not to bend your elbows. Remember that the more you let your middle drop, the more efficient the exercise. It's the same as doing a bicep curl in which you extend your arm fully. I need you to completely extend (drop), so that when you go to contract, you have farther to go!

Now, exhale and "pick it up." Without moving your back, see how far you can bring up your belly. Make sure you're coordinating the movement upward with the exhale. If you want to drop it and rest, go ahead; then contract again on the exhale. Make sure you relax fully between each one. See if you can tire your muscles—and even feel a burn. This is a great exhale and abs exercise!

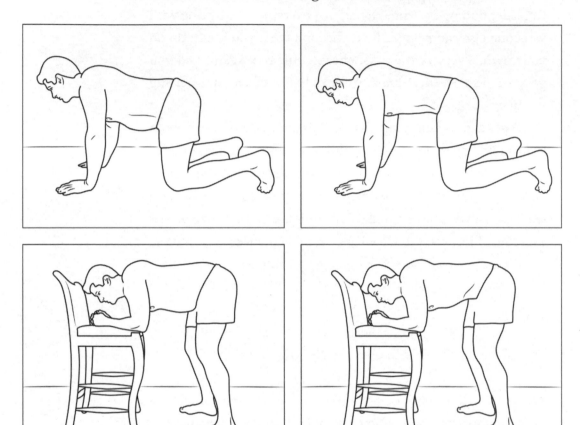

Count how many times you can contract, then work on increasing that number with time. It's easier on the knees when you are leaning on a chair.

FAQ: I can't get my belly to fully release in Tabletop. Any pointers? You've been bracing so long that it's a challenge, I understand. Sometimes putting your hand momentarily above your belly button when you're in this position helps cue you as to where to relax. The fact is, we've gotten so disconnected from our middles that a movement as subtle as this can be very challenging in the beginning.

Balloon Blows

Take a big belly Rock and Roll Breath. Put an empty balloon to your lips. As you roll back to exhale, squeeze your ab muscles and blow into the balloon. This may seem like two separate movements in the beginning, but keep doing them together until it starts to feel natural. It will happen—I promise you! Remember, the first blow will be hard because it's probably a new balloon (and you may be using your cheeks to blow it up). It will get easier.

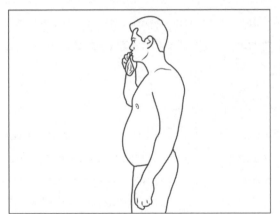 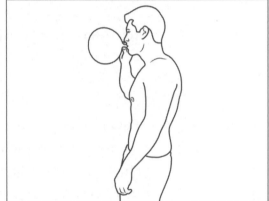

Keeping the balloon in your mouth and not letting the air escape, roll forward, inhaling through your nose. Then exhale into the balloon while tightening your abs to get the air out again. Do not fill your cheeks with air or tighten your neck as you exhale. If you start feeling pressure in your face, get red, or feel light-headed, it means you're trying to use your face and neck to exhale. Exhale only with your exhale muscles: the ones at the middle of your body.

FAQ: I feel like giving up after one breath, after just one balloon. What am I doing wrong? Get a baseline for yourself,

Not using your face or neck is difficult at first. Watch yourself in a mirror—you'll be surprised to see parts of your neck tense up when you thought it was relaxed. Once you get it and keep your cheeks and head out of the movement, it will make sense. At this point, you should continue doing Rock and Roll and filling up the balloon.

because the good news is that you'll get stronger much quicker—even from one day—if you keep track of your progress.

Blowing up the balloon with your belly means that the air goes directly from your belly (or rather, the lower part of your lungs) into the balloon. This is an excellent exhale muscle exercise that you can do once you're good at Exhale Pulsations and actually know how to exhale and squeeze/contract your middle. In essence, you're adding difficulty to the exhale in order to work out your exhale muscles better.

Advanced Balloon Blows

Put an empty balloon in each hand. Blow into one balloon until it's full, and, without changing your rhythm, switch to the empty balloon, while continuing to exercise your exhale muscles. Focus on trying to exhaust these muscles. Feel a slight burn? Good!

Make ballooning part of your workout and praise yourself as these muscles get stronger and the concept gets easier.[33]

Pause now after a Balloon Blow and take a slow, expansive inhale, softening the back of your throat and letting your body relax as you take in air. Notice how much wider and more satisfying your inhale

---

33 As your muscles get stronger, your posture will improve. For more on this, see Kyndall L. Boyle et al., "Clinical Suggestion: The Value of Blowing Up a Balloon," in the *North American Journal of Sports Physical Therapy*.

feels. Think you may even have changed your Vital Lung Capacity? You may have; in fact, retest yourself now.

STEP EXHALES

Your inhale is governed primarily by your diaphragm and intercostal muscles; your exhale is governed by your obliques and other ab muscles. When you learn to recognize which are weaker, you can focus on those areas.

Exhaling out "in steps" works your exhale muscles in a different way, due to the fact that you have to stop several times as you let air out. Think about a movement at the gym: rather than let the weight fall after you curl it, you hold it a quarter of the way down, hold it again halfway down, then three-quarters down just a second more, then you let it go. This is the same concept: Take a big, expansive belly breath, really maximizing the inhale, packing in as much air as you can. Hold it a few seconds, and when you feel as if you need to start exhaling, let out a little air. Then pause. Let out another teaspoon of air. See how long you can draw this out. When you get to the end, you should be leaning back, stomach scooped out—you may even press in your abdomen with your fingers and get the last bit of air out. By the end, it should be challenging. *Whew!* Then tip forward. Inhale.

THE NEXT 14 DAYS—CREATE A WORKOUT FOR YOURSELF

Decide which exercises and stretches you're going to do from the previous chapters: Rock and Roll, Cat and Cow, Inhale and Exhale Maximizations, Exhale Pulsations (regular or in Tabletop), Balloon Blows, Step Exhales, and then stretches. Later you'll add Counting/Patterned Breath and Recovery Breath/Meditation.

Write down your routine and goals. It's been my experience that

DAILY WORKOUT

1. Rock and Roll every hour

2. 25 Exhale Pulsations, 4x a day

3. Cat Cow + Intercostal stretch 2x a day

there's a crucial learning period for relearning how to breathe: fourteen days. Again, as far as your body is concerned, Lower-body Breath (LBB), as you know by now, is not really a brand-new way to breathe. It also makes sense anatomically: when you inhale, your diaphragm should flatten; hence, you're adding anatomical momentum to the learning process. After two weeks of doing these exercises a few minutes a day, they'll become more natural. You'll discover that you're reminding yourself less, and your previous dysfunctional breathing will start to feel unnatural. For some people, this change comes around days seven through ten; for others it takes a little longer. It's important that you commit to the full fourteen days; use whatever method works for you and keeps you on track.

⌒ I never thought exhaling would be so hard. But now I understand: my exhale has been so hard because I haven't been able to take a real inhale. No wonder I have a constant feeling of not getting enough air. For my workout, I do Rock and Roll, focusing on making my inhale bigger and my exhale smaller—you know, Inhale and Exhale Maximization—every hour on the hour. Every other set, I'll do a Step Exhale. Then, three times a day, just for a minute or two, Cat and Cow, Exhale Pulsations, one Balloon Blow, and some stretches. My goals? To do one hundred Exhale Pulsations in a row, twenty-five Exhale Pulsations in Tabletop, and ten Balloon Blows in a row. So while I'm still heavy and nowhere near a flat/neutral or concave stomach, I can already feel my core getting stronger and my inhale is feeling more satisfying because my exhale is better. —Cynthia, age 35

I've always been likened to a beanpole, and though folks think I must be athletic because I'm thin, I actually don't feel like my breathing is good. What I've realized now is that I have barely any inhale. I can exhale, but the inhale gets stuck. I almost have to push my belly out to get that belly breath. I feel like my muscles and lean shape don't let me release the way I should. Relaxing my middle and getting myself to have a more flexible rib cage is what I have to focus on; and each day I feel like I get a little bit better at it. I stop whatever I'm doing and do the series of seated Rock and Roll, Cat and Cow, and Perfect Standing Breath four times a day. In the morning and evening, I really focus on the stretching exercises. When I find myself standing on line I'll do Step Exhales and Exhale Pulsations in a subtle way. Since my goal is to make my inhale better, I really focus on Inhale Maximizations. —Gunner, age 51

Bryan's Story

Bryan had become convinced that he was always going to have trouble sleeping; it was just part of his personality. After taking a class by chance—accompanying a friend—Bryan was tested and identified as a No-haler: his slim frame showed very little change in the inhale and exhale. Bryan focused his workout on the exercises that helped him expand his breath. He slept that night as he never had before. To his surprise, it wasn't just luck. The next day he did as well.

7

POSTURE

Despite being the same person, Superman and Clark Kent adopt very distinct postures. One posture is much like that of a guy spending too much time in front of a computer (or in Clark's case, a typewriter): shoulders rounded, neck jutting forward. Along with the thick horn-rimmed glasses and the stutter, this posture portrays a man lacking in confidence. When changing to Superman, Clark removes his glasses, puffs up his chest, and narrows his gaze. Immediately he oozes strength and assurance. Another caricature that depicts a well-known posture is that of Jessica Rabbit. This is a common "selfie" pose for women: butt tilted out, gut sucked in, breasts jutting forward.

Now let's talk about *your* posture. You vacillate between hunched over the wheel or cell phone and a stiff "social" pose. You know your posture is bad but probably have shied away from addressing it because you don't know where to start. Maybe if you ignore it, you hope, it will fix itself or go away, right? Wrong. The bad news is that poor posture is not only affecting your skeleton, it's also impacting the most important thing you do: your breathing.

Oxygenating and balancing your breath means you're addressing your health at the root, not just bandaging the symptoms. If you really want "wellness," you need to go back to basics and make sure the foundation of your health—your breathing—is good.

The good news is that I'm going to give you the CliffsNotes for fixing your posture, or at least making it way better than it is now.

Consider this: poor posture can affect your ability to breathe by up to 30 percent.[34] Think about that: *30 percent*. That's one-third of all the other good work you're doing down the drain. If you're wondering how the position of your head, neck, shoulders, and back can have such a colossal effect on respiration, the answer is pretty simple: Your head alone is pretty darn heavy. And when your body isn't supporting it as well as it should, the rest of your physical functions get thrown out of whack big time.[35]

FORWARD HEAD POSTURE (FHP) OR, AS IT'S COLLOQUIALLY CALLED, "TEXT BACK"

Even if your body is in decent shape, it doesn't mean that your breathing is in top form. The same goes for your posture. You may have abs of steel, bulging biceps, and to-die-for delts, but if your skeleton isn't properly aligned, these muscles—as well as your diaphragm,

---

34 Rene Cailliet, M.D., author of a series of books on musculoskeletal medicine and former Director of the Department of Physical Medicine and Rehabilitation at the University of Southern California, has pointed out that "forward head posture (FHP) may result in the loss of 30% of vital lung capacity. These breath-related effects are primarily due to the loss of the cervical lordosis, which blocks the action of the hyoid muscles, especially the inferior hyoid responsible for helping lift the first rib during inhalation" (*The Rejuvenation Strategy*).

35 While coming out of the stiff Superman pose may seem easy, this stance is pretty deeply ingrained: The study "It Hurts When I Do This (or You Do That)," by Vanessa K. Bohns and Scott S. Wiltermuth in the *Journal of Experimental Social Psychology*, reported that by simply adopting more dominant poses, people feel more powerful, in control, and able to tolerate more distress. Also see Amy Cuddy, *Presence: Bringing Your Boldest Self to Your Biggest Challenges* (New York: Little, Brown, 2015).

core, and other breathing muscles—aren't working as well as they could or should be.

Do you spend a little too much time on Facebook, Instagram, or whatever the latest social media is? Are you an office drone at your day job? Do you spend more than two hours a day behind the wheel? Do hours pass by as you're hunched over your laptop or iPad? If you said *yes* to one or more of these questions, then your posture just isn't up to snuff, no matter how hard you're working out at the gym.

Yes, your cell phone could be seriously messing with your posture, and that's nothing to LOL at. It's all because of something called Forward Head Posture, or FHP. Ever heard of "Text Back"?[36] You will, because FHP is a problem of modern life, and it's not going away anytime soon. FHP occurs when your head is positioned so that your ears are *in front of* your shoulders instead of directly above them. In comparison, ideal posture means that your head is positioned with your ears over your shoulders, your shoulders are aligned with your pelvis, your pelvis is over your knees, and your knees are over your ankles.

The effects of technology on your posture are hardly exaggerated. Texting places your head an estimated 4.5 inches past your shoulders. And according to chiropractors and other experts, for every inch your head moves forward, *a whopping 10 pounds in weight are added to your upper back and neck muscles.*[37] That's because these muscles have to work much harder to support your head to keep it from dropping onto your chest. It also causes your suboccipital

---

36 New Zealand physiotherapist Steve August calls it "the iHunch" and Harvard professor Amy Cuddy calls it "the iPosture" ("How iPhones Ruin Your Posture and Your Mood" in the *New York Times*, December 13, 2015).

37 According to Dr. Ibrahim A. Kapandji, for every inch your head moves forward, it gains 10 pounds in weight as far as the muscles in your upper back and neck are concerned (*Physiology of the Joints*, vol. 3). This also forces the suboccipital muscles (they raise the chin) to remain in constant contraction.

Are you a rib-gripper? Bad news. This means you're constantly tucking your ribs in, creating a narrowing at the bottom of your rib cage, which makes it harder to take a full breath. Check out the work of Canadian physiotherapists Diane Lee and Linda-Joy Lee for more information.

muscles, which support the chin, to be in constant contraction, which then puts pressure on the related nerves. All told, FHP can add some 30 pounds of work to your cervical spine, throwing your whole skeleton out of alignment.

To get an idea of how this feels, hold a 10-pound kettlebell directly over your head. Now, bending at the shoulder but keeping your arm straight, hold it at 45 degrees. The weight suddenly feels a lot heavier, doesn't it? Well, this is exactly what happens when you lean your 10-pound noggin forward. Just think of how that can affect your spine and muscles over many years. It's no surprise, then, that FHP can exacerbate old neck, shoulder, and back injuries, and also cause TMD (temporomandibular joint disorder).[38]

Sounds pretty unpleasant, right? But your skeleton and musculature aren't the only things affected by poor posture. In fact, FHP blocks the action of your hyoid muscles, the ones that lift your ribs during inhalation. As a result, you squeeze your lungs and other organs into a cramped position that limits the ability of your diaphragm to do its job. You take shallower and less efficient breaths and, consequently:

- You underutilize your full lung capacity due to FHP, which means that, even if you exhale completely and take a big in-

---

38 For a rather long but highly readable article on how the jaw system and the postural system are connected, go to http://www.portlandtmjclinic.com/tmj -disorders/the-role-of-body-posture/.

hale, you still only fill about two-thirds of your lungs with fresh oxygenated air.

- Poor posture actually *weakens* your breathing muscles because of all the strain under-breathing imposes on your body.[39]

Now let's fix these important parts of your body.

IMPROVING YOUR POSTURE: FHP

The first step: Get a picture of yourself from the side, both sitting and standing. Take a look: Is the back of your head in line with your spine? Or is your head leaning forward, your back curved? Now, make a few adjustments. "Tuck" your chin by pushing it back

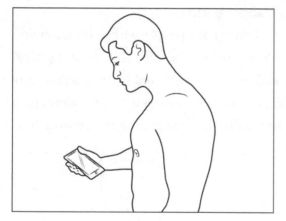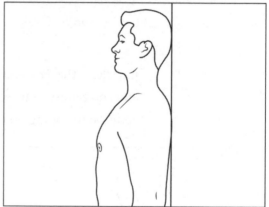

[39] For one of many articles published on the effects of FHP (e.g., chronic pain conditions and other health problems, including tension headaches, increased blood pressure, disc herniation, arthritis, pinched nerves, eye and ear dysfunction, fibromyalgia, upper back pain, and reduced shoulder mobility) see Dan Vaughn, "Looking Forward," *Journal of Manual and Manipulative Therapy* 21, no. 4 (2013): 175–76.

The postural muscles are there to support you and to maintain the appropriate curve of the spine. The postural muscles of the shoulder include the pectoral muscles (which act internally to rotate the shoulders), the levator scapulae, upper trapezius, scalenes, subscapularis, and suboccipitals. The postural muscles of the trunk include the cervical, thoracic, and lumbar erector spinae muscles. Their job (and to a lesser extent, that of the abdominals) is to extend the spine and keep you erect. In the pelvis and thighs, the postural muscles include the hamstrings, psoas, quads, adductors of the leg, and piriformis.

slightly, so that your ears are directly over your shoulders. Take another picture and notice the difference.

IMPROVING YOUR POSTURE: YOUR SHOULDERS

The second step in adjusting and improving your posture is to look at the position of your shoulders. When standing with your back against the wall, your shoulder blades should lie flat against the wall. Be careful not to billow out your chest in order to achieve this. Just slide your shoulder blades together.

Often I see people with rounded shoulders, due to the fact that their pectoral muscles—the *Pectoralis majors*—are constricted (thanks again, cars and computers). The solution: deep tissue massage and stretching, in addition to rolling on tennis balls, then graduating to a lacrosse ball.

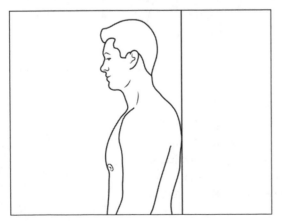 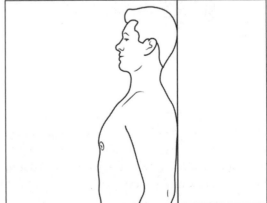

IMPROVING YOUR POSTURE:
YOUR PELVIS

Now put one hand behind you in order to gauge how much space there is between the curve of your lower back (lumbar) and the wall. There should be just enough to allow you to slide your hand through easily. Too much space? Tilt your hips forward to narrow it. Too tight a squeeze? Tilt your butt back so that you create more curve at the back of your spine.[40]

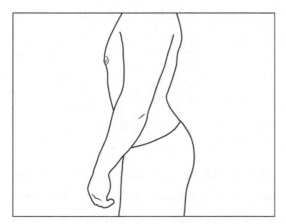 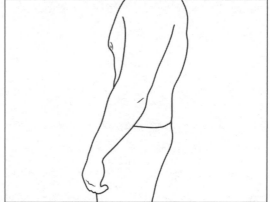

Need help? Tilting your pelvis can be a hard concept, so try lying on the floor and adjusting your hips so that your lower back is pressing into the floor. Conversely, this is a good way to achieve a "posterior pelvic-tilt." To a certain extent, it's similar to the position you assume when you're slouched on a couch. Tipping your pelvis back is the position you take when you're about to do a squat at the gym, arching your back—the same position as used in Cow.

40 For more detail on the subject of the neutral spine, see Nigel Palastanga and Roger Soames, *Anatomy and Human Movement: Structure and Function* (London: Churchill Livingstone, 2012).

Work those pecs. Put your shoulder blades flat on the wall. Hard to do? The *Pectoralis major* is the powerful internal rotator of the arm that can cause the shoulders to be pulled down and in toward the chest. Rule of thumb: when a muscle is "tight" or increased in tone, work or exercise the opposing muscle; in the case of tight pecs, work the external rotators of the shoulder.

Too often, when people think about good posture, about lengthening their spine, they try to stretch upward and consequently pull in their stomachs, inadvertently falling back into dysfunctional Vertical Breathing. Try doing it right: keep yourself belly breathing while reaching upward with the crown of your head. Feels different, right?

See if, when standing against the wall, your back and head are both touching the wall. Performing this alignment will make you feel as if you're leaning back; it's the result of having leaned forward for so long. In addition to having your head touch the wall, put your hand on the back of your neck to make sure you're creating length. Do this by practicing, and experiment by moving your chin downward and lengthening your head upward.

WHAT'S YOUR BRAIN GOT TO DO WITH YOUR POSTURE?

The cerebellum is the part of the brain that controls muscle movement, and, consequently, balance and equilibrium. It also helps control eye movement and is responsible for maintaining active postural muscles. As I explained earlier, poor posture is due to a weakness in the muscles that maintain good posture. People who have poor posture may suffer from dizziness or orthostatic hypotension (a drop in blood pressure when getting up hurriedly or turning the head quickly), and feel sick when reading in a car. Old injuries, physical inactivity, a career as a desk jockey, and inborn weakness in the nervous system may affect the electrical output of the cerebellum and all that it controls. Physical activity—more specifically, exercises that create extension—is the quickest way to improve neurological function and, consequently, your posture.

Postural weakness and instability may lead to deterioration of spinal joints and eventually degenerative joint disease (severe arthritis) of the spine.

FIX YOUR OWN WORK SETTING ERGONOMICALLY

If you spend at least thirty-five hours a week in an office, take a serious look at your workspace. Don't wait for new, modern ergonomic

furniture to be delivered from above; *you* can do something about the ergonomics of your work setting.

Your feet should be flat on the ground when sitting; adjust your chair if they're not. When your hands are on the keyboard, the bottom of your arms, wrists, or forearms should be parallel to the floor, while your shoulders are relaxed. *Do not move your shoulders up or down in order to get your forearms to the right place.* If you have a laptop, get a separate keyboard. When sitting up straight, examine your viewing angle. You should not be looking up at your screen; it should be at eye level. The distance should be such that you can read the screen comfortably, without adjustment (i.e., squinting). And if you catch yourself leaning forward to see better, bring the screen in closer; don't move toward it. Make sure you're not leaning forward in an attempt to get your work done faster!

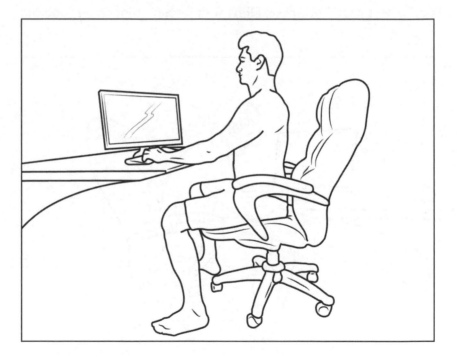

Check your shoulders to make sure they're relaxed and down. Much shoulder pain comes from working at a keyboard that is positioned too high, for which you compensate by raising your shoulders an inch or two. Make sure you relax them and that your desk is accommodating *your* needs. Yes, you may have to move your desk up, add an under-the-desk shelf for your keyboard or a cushion on your chair, but all the changes are worth the effort. *And you definitely are worth it!*

I just read an article in the New York Times about how texting is not only bad for your posture, but also for your mood! So in an attempt to text less, or at least be more thoughtful and less knee-jerky about checking my phone, I made it my rule that I would have to do five Rock and Roll Breaths before looking. Ended up getting a grip on my text addiction and breathing better! —Belle, age 68

I always thought that sitting up against the back of my chair, be it at work or in the car, was good for my posture. But now as I try to Rock and Roll, I realize I can't really tip back. Sure, "perching" and not touching the back feels peculiar at first, but actually bumping my butt back meant that my spine was more stabilized. Now breathing is making my back and abs move and get involved. For the first time ever, my lower back feels good—I thought I was going to have to learn to live with the pain. —Brinkley, age 34

8

BACK AND FRONT

YOUR BACK

Your whole body breathes, and your whole body is positively affected by your breath *when you breathe right*. So first, let's talk about your back (the spine and muscles that accompany it—see figure 6), and then we'll move on to the front (your digestive organs and everything related to breaking down food, from the cellular to the mechanical).

Breathing with the lower part of your body—Horizontal Breathing—is *essential* to your back health. Dysfunctional breathing causes neck and shoulder pain, mid-back pain and tightness, and can cause lower back and pelvic-floor discomfort, as well as bulging and herniated discs.

Your diaphragm and back are irrevocably linked, as the diaphragm's ligaments connect to your spinal column at both the thoracic (T12) vertebrae and your lumbar (L1 and L2) vertebrae, joining it to both the middle and the lower back. The ramifications of associative problems are extensive. A study in the *Clinical Journal of Pain* concluded that breathing problems increased the risk of back pain and vice

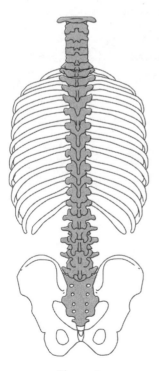

Figure 6

versa.[41] Stress in the body raises cortisol in the muscles and therefore places strain on the back through excess diaphragm tension. What this means is that negative emotions (sadness, anger) hurt your back.

Conversely, research shows that low-back pain has a drastic impact on how you breathe; it reduces the size of the diaphragm and raises it in the chest cavity so that your breath becomes shallower. In fact, the diaphragm is much more easily fatigued in people with back pain, causing faster, shallower breathing, contributing to overall fatigue, and trapping you into a loop of pain and fatigue.

Stop scowling! A study conducted by Daniel McIntosh and his colleagues in the journal *Cognition and Emotion* purports that facial expressions can alter the volume of air inhaled though the nose, which in turn influences brain temperature and affective states.

Breathing dysfunctionally restricts the body flexibility that keeps joints lubricated and muscles supple (through flexion and blood flow). The spine doesn't get the requisite movement, pressure, and support of the breath with every inhale and exhale (which is why you keep feeling as if you need back support from a chair back or compressive garments). The muscles of the pelvis and the pelvic floor are restricted in their range of motion, which leads to pelvic-floor imbalance and lower-back discomfort.

The concept that tension—both physical and emotional—causes back pain (and disease) is not new. Dr. John E. Sarno has given the

---

41 Several recent studies (e.g., Catherine Woodyard, "Exploring the Therapeutic Effects of Yoga and its Ability to Increase Quality of Life," *International Journal of Yoga* 4, no. 2 [2011]: 49–54) have shown that breathing exercises, when combined with yoga and meditation, reduce pain and emotional symptoms 2.5 times more effectively than physiotherapy exercise even with additional counseling and therapy. Breathing, yoga, and meditation were 1.5 times better at returning mobility to chronic low-back pain sufferers.

Vertical Breathing means you're overusing neck and shoulder muscles (front *and* back of body), which then throws the balance of muscles off all the way down your body. And it really does throw your balance off—your natural center of gravity is right below your belly button. You aren't imagining it; the feeling of being more balanced when you breathe low is real; your center of gravity gets lower, you are both physically and emotionally more balanced as a consequence.

The self-massage that comes with the wavelike motion of breathing with your entire body is not only beneficial for gastric peristalsis, but has a very precise calming effect on your neurological system.

name "Tension Myositis Syndrome" to the pain that comes when cells and tissues get less and less oxygen and therefore experience pain.[42] There is a tightening from your chin down to the bottom of your pelvis, with an accompanying domino effect in dysfunction. Better inhales and exhales are part of the solution; addressing stress levels (and even deeper, subconscious emotional pain) is a big part of the cure.

Taking Care of Your Back: Diaphragm Extensions

Moving the pelvis to jut out the belly is a slightly less expansive breath than keeping the back flat on the floor. I've found that the sway that comes with that movement helps dismantle the rigidity in the middle of the body that has been caused by a Vertical Breath.

Try these two subtle but advanced exercises.

Diaphragm Extensions with Hip/Back Movement

So now that you know how to include the lower part of your body in your breathing, go back to lying on the floor and doing Diaphragm Extensions. Finesse the move: On the inhale, soften your

---

42 Sarno is a leader in recognizing that musculoskeletal disorders are frequently caused by a complex interaction between the mind and the body, and his *Healing Back Pain: The Mind-Body Connection* is a *New York Times* bestseller.

glutes, hips, pelvic floor, and thighs. Notice how naturally your hips tip. Exhale, give your lower abs, pelvic floor, and glutes a little squeeze, and notice how your hips tip under and the space between your lower back and the floor narrows. Then exaggerate the rhythm. You'll find that the movement in your hips, though subtle, is quite natural and goes along with the breath.

Diaphragm Extensions without Hip/Back Movement

Once you feel as if the hip movement is really solidified in your head, try leaving your back completely still and flat against the floor, not moving your hips, and just expanding your belly to inhale and exhale. Notice how different this feels.

With both exercises, you're focusing on the front of your diaphragm. Our long-term goal is to have your diaphragm stretch all the way around (it is in fact, roundish!). Use your sides (the parts you stretch in Intercostal Stretch on pages 72–74) and back (the part you stretch in Child's Pose and V-Back Opener on pages 74–75). After working on these stretches and exercises, you'll be able to widen your entire body (not just take a front belly breath) without moving your shoulders (and with no popping-out of your belly, which can make you self-conscious). Your inhale will be wide, and your exhale will be narrow, but the movement will be all the way around your body. It's advanced stuff that will take time, but just keep it in mind as a long-term goal.

THE FRONT: BREATHING AND DIGESTION

How your breathing affects your stomach, your digestion, and pretty much all your intestinal functions has both a cellular and an anatomical component. You need oxygen to digest nutrients at a

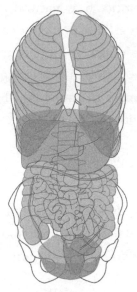
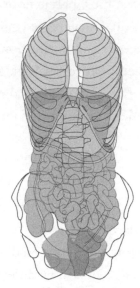

Figure 7
Inhale

Figure 8
Exhale

microscopic level, and you need to breathe well—horizontally, with your diaphragm massaging the organs underneath—in order to have your digestive organs work effectively.

First, let's review the cellular component. At the cellular level, food must be broken down to its chemical components, which include a range of energy-building molecules. Digestion occurs in the digestive tract, and also occurs on a smaller scale within the cell's specialized organelle, the lysosome. Digestion breaks apart the larger molecules such as polysaccharides, fats, and proteins into monomer subunits of sugars, fatty acids, amino acids, and nucleotides, but what does it need to do this well? *You guessed it, oxygen!*

Second, there is the anatomical component. In a nutshell, breathing with your diaphragm will mean fewer GI problems (such as acid reflux, GERD, constipation, and IBS). Why? Well, if you breathe vertically, your diaphragm doesn't massage the organs directly underneath it—your stomach, colon, liver, and kidneys. Switching to Horizontal Breathing means that you're giving your internal organs, especially your digestive organs, a massage with every breath. It's called "peristalsis," the wave-like squeezing motion of the intestines that promotes digestion and elimination. Now, the body already does this normally without any prompting; however, it does it better with help from above (the diaphragm—see figures 7 and 8). If you're breathing with your shoulders (vertically), your diaphragm is barely doing what it should when it comes to digestion. Apart from what you're eating, the biggest factor affecting your digestion of food is how effectively the muscles of your stomach are working. And you guessed it—food isn't getting digested the way it should if you're only running on two cylinders.

Maybe you have a doctor who says, "Ah, irritable bowel! Well, yes, it is a common disorder that affects the large intestine, causing bloating, gas, diarrhea, and constipation, but I can tell you that the main cause is stress." And they might mention that you should learn about diaphragmatic breathing. If they do mention breathing, it's likely because, as you now know, the diaphragmatic breathing helps your digestive muscles do their job, and also because taking Lower-body Breaths makes you calmer.

Fortunately, if you're holding this book in your hands, you're learning all about diaphragmatic breathing, so let me add to your information bucket and take you on a *picnic* that will help your digestion.

DR. BELISA'S BETTER BELLY RULES
FOR ACID REFLUX: P-I-C-N-I-C

- **P**ause before you start eating (you might consider giving thanks for your food).
- **I**f you are about to talk, stop, put your fork down, and talk.
- **C**hew each mouthful at least five to ten times (if you can do twenty, even better). No gulping.

- **No** food or drink that is acidic; e.g., citrus fruits, wine, beef, pickles, processed cheese, or tomatoes.[43]
- **Instead** of going right to bed after eating, grab a piece of gum, and go for a short walk.[44]
- **Consider** sips of aloe drinks throughout the day.

PH AND ACIDITY OF YOUR BODY

The body uses breathing to manage pH, or the balance between the levels of acid and alkaline substances in your body. When your body fluids become too acidic, low-level acidosis causes, among other things, fatigue and pain, while higher ranges cause organ damage or even failure. At the other end of the spectrum, a buildup of alkaline substances in your fluids causes alkalosis, which causes numbness, muscle spasms, and dizziness at low levels, before causing seizures, heart arrhythmia, and coma. It's scary-sounding stuff, but the underlying mechanisms of your body are solidly built in order to keep you functioning well on a pH balance. Those mechanisms rely not on expensive alkaline water, but on your breathing.[45]

According to several studies, you should chew soft foods five to ten times before swallowing, and denser foods (certain vegetables and meats) up to thirty times before swallowing. "Mindful eating," which has roots in Buddhist teaching, advocates that you should spend ten to twenty minutes gazing at your food before grabbing that fork.

---

43 For a comprehensive chart of acidic food by degree, go to http://greenopedia .com/alkaline-acid-food-chart/.

44 This is not your grandmother's remedy. See B. Avidan et al., "Walking and Chewing Reduce Postprandial Acid Reflux," *Alimentary Pharmacology & Therapeutics* 15, no. 2 (2001): 151–55.

45 The rhythm and quality of our breathing affects blood pH levels, making it

FAQ: Can breathing affect the acidity of my body? Yes, because chronic ventilation (over-breathing) at low levels results in an imbalance of carbon dioxide and oxygen. Put some time and effort into your exhale.

Carbon dioxide gets bad press. It's not noxious; in fact, the primary control substance of your body pH is carbon dioxide in the form of carbonic acid and bicarbonate, which equalize the acidity and alkalinity, respectively. The cellular metabolic processes that produce energy require oxygen, which promotes alkalinity, but those energy processes produce carbon dioxide, which is an acid. In order to balance the system, the circulatory system moves the carbon dioxide to the lungs for exhalation.

In application, if the body doesn't get enough oxygen it becomes acidic. Studies show that breathing rates increase as the body attempts to correct pH, and, as a result, blood pressure rises, heart rate elevates, and plasma concentrations of stress hormones surge. The quality of our breath is the key factor in maintaining optimal system balance and preventing both acidosis from not breathing and alkalosis from hyperventilation.

The Quickest Way to Fix Your pH: Exhale!

Humans breathe in oxygen and breathe out carbon dioxide. This process sounds simple, but the details are actually quite complex. During the process of breathing, humans convert sugar into energy. Carbon dioxide is a waste product of this process. Carbon dioxide is released into the blood, travels to the lungs, and is exhaled. Because carbon dioxide is a weak acid, the more carbon dioxide in the blood, the more acidic the blood becomes. Still confused? The super-simple version is that if you don't exhale well, you will become too acidic.

---

more alkaline or acidic, and altered pH can correlate with affected pH levels. It is the long-term patterns of respiration and pH level that are of concern. (Maria Perri, "Rehabilitation of Breathing Pattern Disorders," in *Rehabilitation of the Spine: A Practitioner's Manual*, ed. Craig Liebenson. [Philadelphia: Lippincott Williams & Wilkins, 2007.])

FAQ: Can I test my own acidity? Yes, get yourself some acidity test strips at the drugstore and test yourself throughout the day. Get an average for both urine and saliva, since readings can fluctuate.

CRAVINGS, CORTISOL, AND AIR HUNGER

Did you know that stress gives you belly fat? (Even baboons get muffin top when they're stressed out in the wild!) Stress very well might be the reason for the plateau in your diet. Yes, you and your best friend may both be following a new diet, yet your friend will be losing pounds and you will slowly, painfully, be losing ounces. Then you hit that dreaded plateau of eat less, work out more, and get stuck at the same weight. Sound familiar? The one factor you haven't taken into account is your *cortisol level*. If you have a higher level of that stress hormone in your body than she does, it's going to be harder for you to lose weight.[46] That "stress weight" tends to accumulate and stick like glue to your middle. And again, maybe you can't change the stressor, but you can change your reaction—that is, your breathing, which will tell your body to calm down.

Four pointers to help you on your way:

1. The body awareness you gain with meditation and breathing means better control of cravings and impulse eating. How often have you suddenly become ravenous, then made really bad food choices? Quite a few times, right? Your new body awareness will send up red flags to keep you from finding yourself at a drive-

---

46 *Why Zebras Don't Get Ulcers* by Robert Sapolsky explores other fascinating effects of stress. The PBS special, "Stress: Portrait of a Killer" highlights his research, which was conducted on baboons in Africa. It is viewable on YouTube: http://www.youtube.com/watch?v=eYG0ZuTv5rs.

through with a lap full of something greasy that's going to guilt you for the rest of the day.

2. You've heard that folks find it hard to differentiate hunger from thirst. Ever heard of "air hunger"? If you don't breathe well, you'll experience a sensation of not getting enough air into your body. Breathing exercises can help you feel satiated, and thus be instrumental in helping you develop healthier eating habits. While breathing can't get in the way of a full-throttle binge of devouring an entire pizza or quart of ice cream, it can start chipping away at the feeling of "wanting more" that often spearheads bad food choices.

3. The second biggest receptor site for serotonin—that "feel good" neurotransmitter that we all need—is your gut. So if you're bumming and eating for emotional reasons, the solution is to address both your symptoms of depression and anxiety as well as to adopt a diet/exercise plan so that you can experience success, not yo-yo dieting. While you may consider medication and therapy, meditation and breathing calms your body within minutes.

4. Finally, breathing exercises give you a stronger core, and the result is stronger abs and less shame around your belly. More self-love and less self-hate means you will find it easier to feed yourself in a way that is more thoughtful and loving.

9

THE DIAPHRAGM'S COUNTERPART

THE "BOTTOM OF THE CONTAINER": THE PELVIC FLOOR

Many people think that only women who have given birth vaginally have to deal with pelvic-floor issues. Not true. Everyone has a pelvic floor, and it's much bigger, more complex, and way more important than most people think.

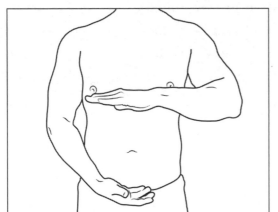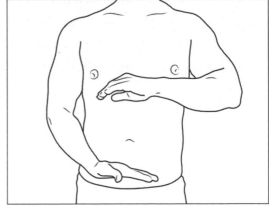

First of all, we're not talking about just one muscle: *there are twenty muscles that make up and/or support the pelvic floor.* And you'd never guess who has the most pelvic-floor issues:

Long-distance runners

Smokers and chronic coughers

People who are chronically constipated

Weight lifters and CrossFitters

People who are overweight

Confused about where the pelvic floor is? Let me guide you.

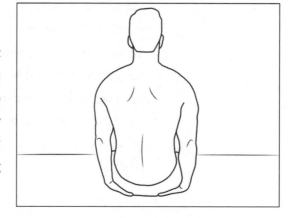

- First, put your hands under your butt and sit on them. You'll feel what are called "bony landmarks," the two pointy bones that press down into your hands. Pull your hands away until only the tips of your fingers are touching these bones—these are your "sitz" bones. Try to imagine how much distance is between them—it might be 4 or 5 inches, or it might be 6 to 8.
- Now, place two fingers of one hand on your pubic bone and two fingers of the other on your coccyx (the tailbone). Your pubic bone is where your zipper ends, and the coccyx is where you'd have a tail, if you had one. If you measure underneath, from front to back, how many inches would it be, 6, 7, 8?

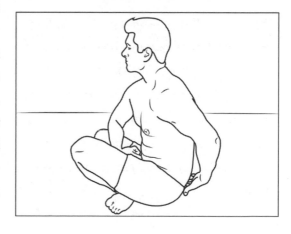

- Think of these two "lines" as intersecting lines that show you a span of space on your body—the size of a very small pizza! Aha! this is the size of your pelvic diaphragm. It's almost the size of your thoracic diaphragm! Maybe they have something to do with each other? Actually they do, very much so, *when you're breathing right.*

Well then, you might ask, where are all those twenty muscles we mentioned earlier? Your pelvic floor relies on muscles in your lower back, your abs, your hips, and all the ones that circle in and out and around your pelvis. And while it's important to be able to locate and distinguish the specific ones that touch the "bicycle seat" (the small pelvic floor), working out the ones that connect to and help them are just as important. Be mindful that your pelvic-floor muscles are deep muscles and, accordingly, you won't feel the burn as you would with more superficial muscles after a workout. You need to pay attention to them, regardless.

Trying to "find" those pelvic-floor muscles? Next time you're urinating, stop in midstream. Those are definitely not *all* the muscles of your pelvic floor, but they can start giving you more awareness of your pelvic floor. *Now don't do this as your exercise; do this just to gain awareness.*

At this point, you should be able to imagine, in your mind's eye, how your pelvic diaphragm is the "bottom" of a container. Your belly and upper abs are the middle of the container, and the top is your thoracic diaphragm. Some people envision a poster tube, others a long water balloon.

There's a muscle that connects the top and bottom of the container—the psoas—and a lot of important organs in between.[47] Good breathing means that both diaphragms move in a rhythm, in synch, and everything between the two really appreciates the massage that occurs with every breath (and conversely, gets very unhappy and sick if it doesn't).

So, here's the rule: Stretch and strengthen. Stretching and lengthening the muscles and moving the joints in your pelvis are absolutely necessary in your daily routine. You need to do both. Many times, a weak pelvic floor is one that is tight and rigid, so doing more contractions (Kegels) isn't going to help and might *exacerbate* any pain you have.

How do I include this in my breathing? Well, if you breathe with a Lower-body Breath, you already automatically are doing it. On the inhale, you should (as in Cat and Cow), relax your belly and hips. What else relaxes when you relax your belly and hips? All the pelvic-floor muscles. *Be careful; I don't mean bear down, I simply mean relax.* Exhale, squeeze your abs, and rotate your hips. Now, each time you tip forward and back, these muscles will contract and expand a minuscule yet significant amount.

Want to take it up a notch? On the exhale (see figure 10), squeeze your lower abs, and then think about squeezing the ab muscles that continue down under your body into a pelvic-floor contraction (or Kegel). Make sure you give an equally important conscious release on the inhale (see figure 9). Now you'll truly get the sensation of how breathing is something your whole body does, and from which your whole body benefits.

---

47 The best explanations and visuals for the complex psoas muscles are provided by the very erudite Tom Myers. See https://www.anatomytrains.com/news/2013/01/20/cobra/.

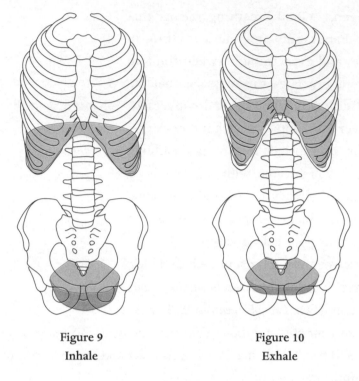

Figure 9   **Figure 10**
Inhale   Exhale

DO THIS

While sitting in a squat or squat variation, put one hand on your bicycle seat (or small pelvic floor). Inhale and feel a slight drop into your hand. Exhale and see if you can pull your pelvic floor off your hand slightly. The movement is small, so you'll only feel a slight difference in pressure on your hand. Good job!

> *FAQ: I'm having a hard time understanding the idea of "relaxing" my pelvic floor. Any suggestions?* Think about when you run to the bathroom and have to pause to let the stream of urine start.
>
> *FAQ: How do I stretch my pelvic-floor muscles?* Sit in a squat as often as possible (or a partial squat, if you have knee

pain). Bear in mind that stretching a muscle is vital to blood flow and its ability to get stronger.

FAQ: I've done Kegels but never added the breath. Remind me how to add the breath. When you contract your pelvic floor, you should be exhaling, which makes sense anatomically. When you inhale, relax your pelvis and hips.

Checklist

- Make sure you relax between squeezes and do a Reverse Kegel, which means softening these muscles. *Don't push down; just let them go.*
- Many of your pelvic-floor muscles are connected to your lower back. Got lower-back pain? Go see a *pelvic-floor* physical therapist.
- Tightening your glutes or thighs is *not* doing a pelvic-floor contraction. Whereas your glutes are important to a healthy pelvic floor and hips, what we want is to focus on the muscles underneath.

Finally, one of the great benefits of all of this is that you align your body with your breathing: that is to say, *you connect with your center of gravity* by moving it down to where it should be, right under your belly button. The lowest, most balancing breath you can take includes your pelvic-floor muscles. When you breathe this "low," you lower your center of gravity; consequently, you are indeed more stable.

FAQ: It's hard for me to imagine both the top and the bottom working together. Can you explain it again? On the inhale, you let your thoracic diaphragm flatten and your pelvic diaphragm relax; then, when you exhale and squeeze, you contract your pelvic diaphragm. It's complex, but the good news is that if you're doing a Lower-body Breath and adding some hip movement, you're already doing a gentle version of this.

Now pause a moment, and look to see how incredibly different this is from breathing with your shoulders. It's like day and night!

Good morning!

At first, I was just bracing my middle when I was exhaling. I had to really retrain myself to exhale and narrow my middle. Lying on my back and exhaling until my belly felt concave helped a lot. It was really about using totally different muscles! Every once in a while during my breathing workout, I'd throw in some Cat and Cow, since that really had that "scooped-out" belly that meant a good exhale. The first week I had to go slow, since I'd get out of rhythm fast. If I didn't pay attention, I'd end up doing a bunch of pulsations totally backward. It's funny, with this whole process, how you have so many "aha!" moments. You just turn a corner and get it. Your body really does want to breathe this way. —Brinkley, age 34

I found I was moving my back a lot when I was doing Exhale Pulsations. When I would get tired, I'd start bouncing my shoulders to inhale and exhale. I had to be stern with myself: Slow down and do them right! This is an abs exhale exercise! It was funny, when doing them right, I felt my abs right away! The next day, I was actually sore all around my middle. But it was a good sore: work your muscles and get it right. It made me proud that I was making such a big change in something so important, this late in life. —Coco, age 55

Gavin's Story

Gavin didn't really think changing his breathing would help, but he came to class to appease his wife, who was worried about his level of stress at work and how it was affecting him. A forty-one-year-old corporate professional, he was having trouble getting to sleep at night, due to the "chatter" in his head about his to-do list. Then, when he finally did fall asleep, he woke up too early—often in a panicky state—feeling tired but with no chance of going back to sleep. The sleep deprivation was making him irritable and short-tempered at work. It took him half the weekend to relax, only to get anxious on Sunday night because of the upcoming week. He stated animatedly that he was not the type to meditate and in the past had either fallen asleep or been restless and annoyed during traditional meditation. It was too "crunchy" and "woo-woo" for him. He wanted nothing to do with "the universe, chakras, chanting, or divine spirits." Hopeful but somewhat skeptical, he learned how his "modern predatory state" at work, crouched over the computer, was burning him out. Not coincidentally, it was the same posture he had while driving and playing golf—shoulders internally rotated, hips tucked under, sunken-in chest. His posture was severely affecting his breathing. Altering his breathing helped ease his constant feeling of exhaustion and changed his ongoing fight or flight mode. He added five minutes of breathing exercises to his morning, midday, and evening routine. His sleep improved as well as his mood.

10

YOUR BREATHING BRAIN

Twenty percent of the oxygen you breathe is used by your brain. Let that sink in for a minute. While it doesn't sprint, do Cross-Fit, or pole-dance, that 10-pound blob in your skull *eats up 20 percent of the oxygen you breathe.* That's pretty intense, and if you don't breathe well, it will surely affect your endurance in your workouts. But it will also affect much more, er, mind-blowing things, like memory, productivity, judgment and, yes, the balance of hormones and neurotransmitters necessary for optimum mental health.

Sit tight; we're going to talk about detoxing your brain, keeping it young, and the truth about nose versus mouth breathing.

FLEX YOUR BRAIN

Get your breathing on, and by the end of this book you'll have:

- a larger hippocampus (for learning, cognition, memory, and emotional regulation)
- a heftier temporoparietal junction (for perspective, empathy, and compassion)
- a sturdier brain stem (the pons, where regulatory neuro-transmitters are produced)

So, let's say this a different way: remembering your PIN, trouble-shooting, multitasking, organizing yourself, organizing others—all of these activities need oxygen, *cell fuel*, to work correctly. And vice versa. So, is your brain not working quite right? You might be low on fuel.

Yikes! Deep breath. So what do I do, doc, you ask? My answer is that you need to add a short breathing/meditation/mindfulness practice to your day. And before you judge and assume that you need a yoga mat and incense, all I'm talking about is taking a few minutes to pay attention to your breath . . . which is, in essence, meditation (which is, yes, being mindful). Having a breathing routine or at least knowing about breathing and taking a couple of seconds a day to focus on it, *is being mindful.*

Perhaps you're going to say one of the two following things: "I don't have time" or "I'm one of those people who can't meditate." But what if I told you that every time you pay attention to your breath—and I do mean just a few seconds of hearing and feeling it go in and out of your body—you're practicing mindfulness? Do it for a few minutes and it *is* meditation—it's as simple as that. And while it might be nice to have a special room in your house where you can perform daily meditation rituals throughout your day, all you have to do is take one baby step—and it might end up being just right for you.

If you're trying to be healthier, wanting to live longer and better, or wanting to heal, you must have a meditation or mindfulness component on your to-do list.[48] Period. Recent research has been confirming this conclusion with ever more evidence as chemical changes, physical brain volumes, and meticulously set physiological markers are tracked and recorded.[49]

---

48 A thought-provoking Web site with an eye-catching name, *Elephant Journal *it's about the mindful life,* offers many articles of interest on green wellness, food, yoga, and, of course, mindfulness and meditation.

49 A report published in 2013 stated that "participants in the mindfulness

Here's cool research: People who were trained in mindfulness had lower pain sensations than people treated with morphine. Researchers at Wake Forest Baptist Medical Center found significant reductions in long-term pain for fibromyalgia patients, as well as reductions in incidences of depression and emotional exhaustion.

BREATHING ISOMETRICS: YOUR COUNTING PATTERNED BREATHING

Slow breathing isometrics help lengthen your concentration and focus, and are in themselves a form of meditation. They also force you to control your muscles over longer periods of time thereby developing your breathing in a subtler but important way. Add counting breath practice to your routine; the goal should be to do this breathing for a specific length of time, and then increase the time as you become more confident of your technique.

Do This:

- Tactical Breathing: This is an exercise I demonstrate in class, one that's used in the military to induce calm.[50] Inhale for 4 counts, then hold for 4 counts, exhale for 6 counts, and hold for 2 counts. Repeat.
- Coherent Breathing joins your heartbeat and your breath. Intuitively, it makes sense: they should be "talking to" and in line with each other (see figure 11). You want to aim for 5 to 6 breaths a minute (with a resting heart rate of about 60). If

---

intervention group experienced significantly less emotional exhaustion and more job satisfaction than participants in the control group." (Ute R. Hülsheger et al., "Benefits of Mindfulness at Work: The Role of Mindfulness in Emotion Regulation, Emotional Exhaustion, and Job Satisfaction," *Journal of Applied Psychology* 98, no. 2 [2013]: 310–25.)

50 http://www.med.navy.mil/sites/nmcphc/Documents/health-promotion -wellness/psychological-emotional-wellbeing/Combat-Tactical-Breathing.pdf.

you inhale for 5 seconds and then exhale for 5 seconds, your body parts are working in unison, in harmony. This type of breathing promotes optimal health and the synchronicity of your body (heart rate variability).[51]

Whichever count makes you happy, the most important part is that the breath be a Lower-body Breath, and that you focus on the exhale being *thorough and long*.

Want to calm down even further?

1. Hum on the exhale (or as some people like to do, sigh).
2. Maintain your rhythm by using a metronome app, your own heartbeat, or music with a beat.
3. Tip forward and back (Rock and Roll Breath) as you inhale and exhale, which adds a really mesmerizing rhythm.

Some variations by people you may know:

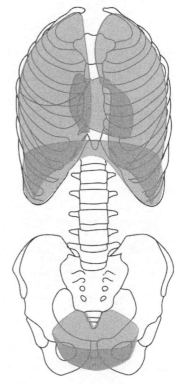

Figure 11

1. Tony Robbins: Inhale for a 5-count, hold the breath for a 20-count, and exhale for a 10-count (and do this 3 times a day).
2. Mark Divine: Inhale for 5 seconds, pause and hold for 5 seconds, exhale for a controlled 5 count, and pause on the exhale for 5. Repeat. You can also choose a 4-count or a 6-count (often called "Box Breathing"; See his book, *Unbeatable Mind*).
3. Al Lee and Don Campbell: Inhale through your nose for 3 seconds. Purse your lips and exhale, while letting your cheeks inflate. Draw the exhalation out to a count of 10, or as long as you're able. Try to get every last bit of air out of your lungs (often called "Pressure Breathing").

---

51 You can read more about "Coherent Breathing" and "Total Breath" in *The Healing Power of the Breath* by Richard Brown and Patricia Gerbarg.

I don't like breath counts that have a "pause" or "hold" for patients who are Breath-Holders. If you're a Breath-Holder, pick a breath count without a pause.

Coherent Breathing maximizes the heart rate variability (HRV), a measurement of how well the parasympathetic nervous system is working. Changing the rate and pattern of breath alters the HRV, which causes shifts in our nervous system. A higher HRV is associated with a healthier cardiovascular system and a stronger stress-response system. Breathing at a rate that is close to one's ideal resonant rate—around five breaths per minute—can induce a significant and immediate improvement in HRV.

4. Dr. Andrew Weil: Close your mouth and inhale quietly through your nose to a mental count of 4. Hold your breath for a count of 7. Exhale through your mouth to the count of 8. Repeat cycle (often called "Relaxing Breath").

As in isometrics, slow conscious breathing helps you gain control over your body. Moving a lot of weight with enthusiasm may be good as part of a regular workout, but using your body weight slowly and effectively works critical muscles.

I CAN'T REMEMBER!

There's another important component in this brain-boosting meditation: memory. Memory is the key that connects you to others and establishes your identity. Meditation and mindfulness help to detox your brain, working wonders for the memory parts of the brain, not only thickening them for protection but also reducing free-radical stress, increasing blood flow, increasing oxygen delivery to the brain, boosting memory performance, and preventing memory-related diseases.

FAQ: So my bad breathing is making me spacey? Yes, in so many words. Think about it: You have more stress, less sleep, and less oxygen in your body. Something is going to break. Brain fatigue may indicate the consequences of neurological oxidative stress.

Some of the most impressive effects of stress on the brain are hippocampus atrophy, shrinkage of the hippocampus or prefrontal cortex (the area of the brain unique to humans), and even neural death in some brain regions. The hippocampus, a vital brain region for episodic, spatial, and contextual memory, has many cortisol receptors, which makes it especially susceptible to stress.

Severe stress lasting weeks or months can impair cell communication in the brain's learning and memory regions.[52] Increased stress hormones lead to memory impairment in the elderly, and learning difficulties in young adults.

THE AGING BRAIN

There are many facts, myths, and legends surrounding the effects of aging, some interesting and others downright scary.[53] So here are some to inform you—and hopefully reassure you—about your lungs, oxygen, and how your brain ages:

1. The lungs mature by age twenty-nine, and yes, thereafter, aging is associated with progressive decline in lung function; however,

---

52 An interesting study by a Harvard neuroscientist finds that meditation not only reduces stress, it literally changes your brain: Sara W. Lazar et al., "Meditation Experience Is Associated with Increased Cortical Thickness," *NeuroReport* 16, no. 17 (2005): 1893–97.

53 Dr. Norman Doidge points out that "as we age and plasticity declines, it becomes increasingly difficult for us to change in response to the world" (p. 232); however, his book *The Brain That Changes Itself* presents the theory of "neuroplacity"—the ability of the brain to change and adapt to new circumstances—in a clear and straightforward way. An excellent read.

that doesn't mean there is nothing you can do. You are now taking the steps to better breathing that can help you to decelerate the process.

2. Experts agree that there are four basic changes that affect lung function as aging occurs: a decrease in motor power, a decrease in the elastic recoil of lung tissue, a stiffening of the chest wall, and a decrease in the size of the intervertebral spaces. Again, lung function can be positively impacted by Horizontal Breathing.

3. Exhales become *less* efficient with aging, due to an increase from 25 percent (at 20 years of age) to 40 percent (at age 70) in residual lung capacity, which accounts for a barrel-like appearance in the chest wall.[54]

There are several "scaries" affecting seniors that you'll probably read about in the news, which should ensure that everyone keeps doing breathing exercises every day:

- The structural changes (e.g., chest wall) impair the total respiratory system compliance (the measure of the lung's ability to expand) and can lead to difficulty in breathing.
- "Senile emphysema" occurs when the lungs lose their supporting structure, which causes loss of elasticity in the alveoli.
- An effective cough, important for airway clearance, can be impaired when respiratory muscle strength decreases with age.

---

54 For more on this subject, Gwyneth A. Davies and Charlotte E. Bolton, "Age-related Changes in the Respiratory System," in *Brocklehurst's Textbook of Geriatric Medicine and Gerontology* (Philadelphia: Elsevier Saunders, 2010).

FAQ: My grandmother says she feels like her breathing is fine, but it doesn't seem right to me. Any ideas? You're probably right. Research shows older adults tend to suffer shortness of breath (dyspnea), oxygen deficiency (diminished ventilatory response to hypoxia), and abnormally elevated carbon dioxide levels in the blood (hypercapnia), all of which makes them more vulnerable to ventilatory failure (e.g., heart failure, pneumonia, etc.).

Dementia has many forms and causes, but one of the most common unifying factors among all of the varying forms is oxygen deprivation to the brain. "Oxidative stress" directly affects brain health in dementia patients. Even the degree of dementia can predict the rate of oxygen flow and uptake.

Consequently, breathing, meditation, and exercise impact brain function as they fuel oxygen to the brain and, in turn, support the autonomic systems, cognition, and memory in seniors.

A FEW WORDS ABOUT MOUTH VERSUS NOSE BREATHING

Your brain and body react very differently to whether air comes into your body through your nose or your mouth.

As an everyday breathing style, mouth breathing (unless you're doing these exercises or running hard) is bad. Period.[55] Moreover, mouth breathers tend to lean forward with their head

---

55 Check it out: Paul Chek has four hours of information about this online in his "The Challenges of Mouth Breathing" videos. In 240 minutes you'll be an expert (sort of), too.

and shoulders, which can cause neck and upper thoracic structural dysfunction. Mouth breathing can also disrupt the pH balance of the blood, making it too alkaline. Alkalosis can lead to feelings of apprehension, anxiety, and chronic pain conditions.

Nose breathing, on the other hand, has its own benefits, including increased CO_2 saturation in the blood, which creates a calming effect.[56] In addition, there is the question of protecting the lungs. The nose—not just your nostrils but the passages deep inside—contains structures (turbinated bones and mucus membranes) dedicated to the filtration and conditioning of the air we breathe, which means if you don't use your nose, there's all kinds of bad stuff going *directly* into your mouth and lungs.

> *FAQ: If nose breathing is best, why not start doing the exercises this way?* Since *most* people are nose breathers, switching temporarily to the mouth for these exercises makes you pay attention to the breath. You're less apt to go back to a dysfunctional Vertical Breath if you're breathing through your mouth. Once the Lower-body Breath becomes more natural and your muscles get stronger, you should definitely switch to your nose—at the very least for the inhale.

BOTTOM LINE

If you want your brain to take care of you, you need to take care of it. To meet your daily meditation requirements, either do a

---

56 Coach Lisa Engles sums up the advantages of nose breathing succinctly: Our nose is made to breathe; nasal breathing disarms the body's stress response; and there's a direct correlation between nasal breathing and heart rate (exertion levels). See her book *Breathe Run Breathe*.

Counting Breath mindfulness session for a few minutes (between five and fifteen), or do the more advanced, tough, two-part breath we'll talk about soon. You might find you like one more than the other, or that each makes you feel good in a different way, so you can alternate or do them both every day.

11

ESSENTIAL TO YOUR
BRAIN HEALTH: SLEEP

You can be doing everything right, but if you aren't sleeping well or long enough, your brain will suffer and rebel—which results in more "stupid" injuries, silly mistakes, and life-threatening lapses in judgment.

There's the good news and then there's the bad news. The good news: while most people "ventilate" less while sleeping, at least their style of breathing is better (less Vertical, more Horizontal/Lateral). The bad news: the better style of breathing at night doesn't make up for bad daytime breathing; in fact, it barely nicks the surface of the problem.

So when I talk about sleep, I'm covering several different issues.

If you've been breathing in fight or flight all day, then how can you expect your body to just flip the switch and go to sleep at night? All day, you've been telling your nervous system that it's in code red, and now, just because you decide it's bedtime, you think your body is going to slow down and calm itself enough to turn off as you would a computer. No way. Your body has to enjoy several moments of calm throughout the day in order to get a good chunk of decompression at night.

1. You can't get to sleep because the chatter ("the committee") won't shut up. Your brain won't turn off, and you find yourself getting angry at it.
2. You wake up too early (often in a mild panic state, which I call "slap awake").

3. You wake up intermittently and toss and turn before going back to sleep.

4. You snore (which is a big red flag for apnea, meaning you're holding your breath throughout the night—very detrimental to your health).

Kids have rituals to tell their bodies it's time to go to bed. They need to take a tubby, get into their jammies, and pick out a book. Adults don't have rituals, but if they did, there would be fewer fifth cups of coffee and reduced complaints of insomnia and fatigue around the conference table the next day. Here are some non-negotiables related to "sleep hygiene" that you have to integrate into your evening routine.

1. If you have items on your list such as "I can't go to bed and fall asleep unless the dishes are done," cross them out. You actually might have to "retrain" yourself to be able to leave dishes in the sink—they aren't going anywhere and will be there tomorrow. This is just an example of a perceived "must do" that truly can wait. (You'll learn in the next chapter how to determine when your stress is self-inflicted.)

2. Get mean about your sleep. If your friends or family don't get your polite boundaries regarding your sleep, get nasty. You have my permission.

3. Nix all the buzzing, beeping, and little red/green lights. Be really stealthy about checking—if you do it carefully, you'll probably find there are at least one or two little red lights that signal to your brain it shouldn't turn off completely.[57] Same

---

57 If you really want to find out what those light-emitting diodes (LEDs) are doing to your sleep, check out Kathleen E. West et al., "Blue Light from Light-emitting Diodes Elicits a Dose-dependent Suppression of Melatonin in Humans," *Journal of Applied Psychology* 110, no. 3 (2011): 619–26.

thing with potential buzzing; your average home has a laundry list of things that go off, including beeping when batteries are low.

4. Turn it off. Turn *what* off? *All of it.* If it is a device that needs to be charged or plugged in, if it has a big or small screen, turn it off. The temptation is huge, but set a time at night when all your gadgets turn off, no matter what. The worst thing that can happen is that the next morning at the office you won't be part of the conversation about the talking dog video that got over 20,000 hits while you were sleeping.

5. Many people will tell you they keep their phones on just in case of emergency. Shorten that list of emergency folks by half and then set your phone to ring only if it's one of the select few (after you have told them firmly what your bedtime is).

6. Soft pajamas, classical music? Figure out what your triggers for sleep are. Just remember, they're helpful, not magic. And make sure you heed rule number 4.

Your otherwise demure significant other snores like a freight train at night? Earplugs might be your new best friends. Try different brands to see which ones work for you. Got a big presentation tomorrow? Separate beds or crating for the snoring pooch doesn't mean you don't love them (spouse and pet, respectively); it's just being practical and protective of your stress levels.

FAQ: As I train my body and brain to agree that it's bedtime, will the time I take falling asleep get shorter and shorter? Yes! Just like the active toddler who falls asleep in the car, you can train yourself to go bed as long as you're firm with your rules. While during the first week your pre-bedtime ritual may take an hour, after a month you can get it down to forty-five minutes, and so on. Although that may seem like a lot of time for your brain to "get" that it's bedtime, remember, it's been on high alert for ten hours straight (plus, it's better to take the extra time before bed rather than having an hour or two of tossing and turning later).

FAQ: I'm not a nap person, but I'd like to be. Any suggestions? Often, it's about finding the right time and space, and knowing it's only going to be ten, fifteen, or twenty minutes. Troubleshoot and get creative. Often, just getting away for a few moments from all the different types of information being hurled at you will let you get into a quasi-sleep state that can be a great reboot.

Just Snoring? Think Again

Lobbing a pillow at them may be enough to get your college roommates to roll over and stop snoring. It has been confirmed that the supine sleeping position—sleeping on your back—causes excessive nasal airway pressure that in turn can lead to constriction and snoring. Sleep apnea is a broad condition of disorders that cause pauses (ten to thirty seconds) in breathing during sleep due to cramped airways, leading to oxygen deprivation, interrupted sleep cycles, and lower overall health. Really, it's not *just* snoring.

And it's documented that these disorders have increased dramatically in the last two decades. Critical as well is the fact that this condition also carries risk factors for stroke and serious cardiovascular diseases.

The remedy of choice is forcing air down your pipes with a Positive Airway Pressure (PAP) machine. Mouth guards that create space in the mouth have varying success rates. Losing weight and rolling

REM deprivation causes mild psychological disturbances, such as anxiety, irritability, hallucinations, and difficulty concentrating; moreover, it may cause appetite and aggression to increase.

Did you know that there is no official terminology to distinguish between disparate types of snores? The British Snoring & Sleep Apnoea Association tells us that, nonetheless, "there are differences that are circumstantial, qualitative and—with respect to noise level—quantitative. There are, for example, those 'conventional' snores, which might be emitted by almost anyone at some point, that are in effect rhythmic but somewhat noisy breaths that happen while the person is asleep . . . At the other end of the spectrum are those extremely loud snorts that follow the ominous silence of a sleep apnea . . . [and] are an overt sign of a serious medical condition."

over (prompted by a shove from the other side of the bed or a vibrating sleep position trainer) are often the simple solutions that might improve this very serious problem.

THE VICIOUS CYCLE

Sleep deprivation disrupts the hormones in the body that control appetite. Obesity increases the risk of breathing-related sleep disorders such as snoring and obstructive sleep apnea, which in turn impair sleep quality and contribute to sleep deprivation.[58]

Whether it's insomnia or your (or someone else's) snoring, "bad" sleep can stress you out and make your daytime cortisol level higher. The result: a vicious cycle of sleeplessness and stress.

While you're reorganizing your life to support your new quest for better sleep (by losing weight and training yourself to sleep on your side to overcome your sleep apnea), a daily fifteen-minute meditation that puts you into a deep meditative state can count as a well-deserved and much-needed nap. More important, it immediately lowers your cortisol, so that flipping the switch to sleep at night will be far easier.

---

58 For more on this, see M. F. Fitzpatrick et al., "Effect of Nasal or Oral Breathing Route on Upper Airway Resistance During Sleep," *European Respiratory Journal* 22, no. 5 (2003): 827–32.

Four Steps to Falling Asleep

1. Make sure you've addressed all the sleep hygiene issues spoken about previously.
2. Stop yourself from getting dramatic or fatalistic about your lack of sleep—that will just rile you up. Even if you don't quite believe it, repeat to yourself that rest is almost as good as sleep.
3. Put an eye pillow or bag of rice on your belly and do a hundred belly breaths. You can substitute your favorite calming breath count as well.
4. Listen to the sound of your breath—actually try to make it noisy. Hearing your breathing can help you get to sleep.

The belly breath helped me sleep. I'd put a bag of rice on my belly so that it wouldn't fall and wake me if I fell asleep, and tried to get to one hundred. The first week I got to eighty, the second and third it got faster and faster. I'm now trying to set a new record. —Jennifer, age 54

On Sunday night, I'd lie in bed trying to get to sleep, but my brain would not be able to turn off. I'd run through scenarios, to-do lists, everything about the week ahead of me. As time went by, I'd get more upset at what was left of the night for me to sleep, knowing for sure I'd now be starting Monday tired. Relearning how to breathe and oxygenating myself better during the day, then having a relaxing breathing practice for before getting into bed, has meant that rarely happens anymore. —Santino, age 49

12

WHY "WORK HARD, PLAY HARD" IS HURTING YOU

"WHAT DOESN'T KILL YOU MAKES YOU STRONGER" NO LONGER APPLIES

You complain that you are stressed-out, that you are tired, that you need to relax, but these proclamations are rhetorical. The person next to you probably agrees that they are, too. You share stories and commiserate with friends on the fact that you don't get enough sleep and that you are exhausted. The people you talk to may rotate, depending on the day, but the script is the same. And everyone agrees: your hairdresser, coworker, neighbor, best friend. But now I am putting you on notice: you've been saying the same things for months, even years. Time to address it.

To add to the problem, our society glorifies being busy. The busy person appears important, and multitasking is something you almost feel a competitive urge to get better at. Then you stress out. The solutions are temporary: massage, a bath, a couple drinks. Or sometimes you just wait it out until your next vacation, or you simply chalk it up to the fact that life will not change because this is just how modern life is: stressful.

Which brings us to the adage, "What doesn't kill you makes you stronger."[59] Right? Wrong. The impact of stress can take years off your lifespan, and even if it doesn't, it does diminish the quality of life.

Some folks find the impact of stress on their lives hard to believe. They look around, saying, I feel as stressed-out as everyone else, then they shrug it off. Well, yes, our society has in effect convinced people that a lack of sleep is normal, that not being able to turn off the chatter when they try to fall asleep is normal, and that lying in bed watching news, writing texts, or doing quasi-social things like responding to a Facebook post keeps them current. And then there are the beeping, honking, and buzzing appliances that require immediate attention.

Check your breathing when you are listening to a disturbing news story. Whereas you are nowhere near the event and might never have experienced that trauma, your body tightens and your breathing gets shallow. Worrying has the same effect on your body: it tenses, as if getting ready for a challenge. All this takes energy from your body; all this makes your breathing shallower. Imagine the effect after hours, days, or weeks of living this way. It is time to change that in order to have more energy, to oxygenate and relax your body, and to take better care of it.

Each year, you make some kind of formal or informal pact with yourself that you'll prioritize better. Relax more, stress less. Take care of yourself. Carve out more "me time" in your nonstop schedule. And each year this resolution lasts between seventy-two hours and a week at most, until you stop trying to meditate, keep a journal, take walks, be in "the now," and just go back to what's easiest—being stressed-out.

So how much stress is, in fact, brought on by you? How much

---

59 The saying, "What doesn't kill me makes me stronger," appears in Nietzsche's *Twilight of the Idols*. While pushing yourself to tolerate more chronic stress will not inoculate you against it, stressful events may make you a stronger person. Malcolm Gladwell's latest book, *David and Goliath*, examines the relationship between "remote misses" and extraordinary achievement, and how difficult childhoods can foster strength and lead to lives of outstanding accomplishments—another way of saying that "what doesn't kill you makes you stronger."

Your body and mind can tolerate a certain amount of stress, as long as there's an adequate amount of downtime to rest and recharge. Watching "mindless" TV or spending time on Facebook is not really time out. In fact, for many people, just sitting still without any kind of input (music, background TV, etc.) has become hard to do.

does stress actually drive you? Are you one of those people who did best in school by cramming and writing papers the night before? Do you feel pride in getting more done today than yesterday? If so, then you do have some of the stress addict in you, and if you're succumbing to another one of the common ailments that have to do with stress (e.g., acid reflux, trouble sleeping, fatigue, and anxiety), you may want to reevaluate your perceptions of stress so you will be able to make some real changes.

ARE YOU A STRESS ADDICT?

If the compulsive part of you thrives under stress,[60] and the other part of you knows it's hurting you and is trying to find peace and balance, the addicted side, the one with the strength of years of habit, is going to win. To start to make a change, you need more insight, and a good place to start is by noting which of the following behaviors resonates with you. These are the top ten patterns that define a stress addict:

1. You feel pride in having completed an imposing daily to-do list. Whether it makes you feel like Supermom or just genetically

---

60 According to research in the field, there is "good stress"—which is called *eustress*. For more on this subject, see the works of Hans Selye, a pioneer in the study of stress (in fact, he coined the term *stress*), especially *Stress Without Distress*. He calls stress "the spice of life."

superior to your friends, there is smugness underneath the complaining.[61]

2. You get a rush from running. Whether it's running to the supermarket, the dry cleaners, or the gym, the pressure of coordinating tasks and achieving goals gives you a rush.

3. You get excited about the idea of multitasking and thereby being more efficient. You want to pat yourself on the back when you're able to do four things well at the same time (which can also lead to a love of gadgets that profess to help you multitask better).

4. You feel important. The idea that so many people need you and that your contribution is essential leads you to feeling wanted and useful. Just think of the chaos if you weren't around!

5. Deep down inside, you believe that stress-related problems are brought about by genetics or are accident-related.

6. You feel uncomfortable, worried, and nervous when you don't have something you must do right away. And what you "need" to do becomes absolute.

7. You depend on and look forward to the buzz of a caffeine high.

8. At times, you wish you could survive on less sleep or take a food pill instead of "wasting time" eating and sleeping.

9. You thrive on taking shortcuts and closing the deal, meeting the deadline. You find yourself saying (or thinking), "Get to the point!" more and more often.

10. You find it difficult to be in the present. You're always either planning for the future or mulling about something in the past. When looking at time, it seems to have flown by.

---

61 The Navy SEALs are trained to be "comfortable in chaos" in order to meet unbelievable challenges, but you have not received that training.

If any one of these behaviors rings a bell,[62] it's time for you to change your lifestyle, because they're all part of a larger pattern of stress addiction. That's the bad news. The good news is that if you've gotten this far in this book, you're on the path to changing your life. Read on!

RANK YOUR STRESS

Stress yellow: You're starting to have trouble sleeping because you can't turn off "the chatter." You might have been told that you grind your teeth at night. You think about work long after the day is done. You find yourself grasping for strategies to help manage whatever it is you have to do. The weekend passes away too quickly, and there never seems to be enough "me time." You re-member a time when you were less stressed and maybe happier. You're taking less care of yourself simply because there aren't enough hours in the day.

Stress orange: All the characteristics of yellow have be-come the norm. Plus, now you find yourself irritable, and occasionally experience disturbing episodes such as road rage when you lose control. You snap at people you

---

62 Dr. Peter Whybrow, director of the Institute for Neuroscience and Human Behavior at UCLA, explores the rise of stress addiction and the consequences of what he calls "the symptoms of clinical mania" in his forthcoming book, *The Intuitive Mind: Common Sense for the Common Good.* Two *New York Times* articles, written five years apart, discuss why hypomania is so attractive to the person experiencing it in the workplace: http://www. nytimes.com/2010/09/19/business /19entre.html and http://www.nytimes.com/2005/03/22/health/psychology /22hypo.html.

love, then feel intense guilt. You're often angry with yourself for not getting everything done. You fantasize about vacations or just getting up and leaving town. These fantasies are replaced by those in which you go postal. You may be taking medications to sleep or relax, and are drinking way too much caffeine or energy drinks in order to stay alert during the day.

Stress red: You've been diagnosed with medical problems that are stress-related (e.g., ulcer or migraine). You've been told by your doctor that, as part of your recovery, you must address the stress in your life or you can expect your health problems to be chronic, and that they'll affect your quality of life/lifespan. Your mental or physical health has been impacted by stress, which could be related to your worry over future stress, your trauma of past stress, or your subjective perception of your current stress. You've been diagnosed with an anxiety or depressive disorder, and therapy and/or medications have been recommended. Whereas anxiety or depressive disorders can have physiological bases, stress can significantly worsen both.

If you stay at level yellow for more than a year, orange for more than a few months, or red for more than a few weeks, there can be serious physical and mental health consequences. The number of injuries you'll suffer—because you didn't notice an important detail or were distracted—may

What happens when you experience stress? Powerful hormones are released throughout the body, elevating blood pressure and putting the senses on high alert. Glucose is driven up to the brain and into the muscles. Your evolutionary preprogrammed response is fight or flight. You're probably in a mild to moderate state of fight or flight all the time, as a "normal" thing—but it definitely isn't normal.

Women experience stress with greater intensity than men. They process words and body language more quickly by using both sides of the brain (which predisposes them to multitasking), and have a deeper limbic system, the seat of emotions (which connects one more sensitively in all relationships).

increase. Self-medicating incidents will augment this. Your body's immune system runs amok because stress disrupts the body's ability to heal itself. The time spent on going to appointments and money spent on medications (usually pain medications) will increase.

You may find yourself feeling distanced from and irritated by your spouse, and your relationships with colleagues and supervisors may feel strained. You may find yourself relying more on alcohol to relax. And ultimately, you'll find yourself living less in the present. You'll be nostalgic about a "simple" past you once had, or dream about the more balanced life you hope to have in the future. You may get forgetful, because stress affects the hippocampus in the brain, so it's hard to remember things you once knew perfectly well. Days and months will whiz by.

THE ULTIMATE NATURAL CURE FOR STRESS

Which came first: the anxious, shallow, Upper-body (Vertical) Breathing or the stress? Regardless, you're in the loop. Breathing badly, you feel stressed, and the stress pushes you to breathe worse—you take small, shallow, erratic breaths. This in turn alerts your nervous system to go deeper into fight or flight, which then constricts your breath even more. Are you in a war zone? Nope, just crouched over your computer, growing more impatient and full of anxiety with every hour, stressed about your to-do list, your project deadline, and all the things that demand your immediate attention.

Changing the way you breathe will lower stress levels within minutes. Faster than a Valium, a double shot of scotch, or a good massage. Yes, you yourself can lower your blood pressure faster (and with fewer side effects) than any medication. If you could hook yourself up to a machine that measures galvanic skin response, heart rate, blood pressure, and brain waves within seconds, all the signs that your body is calming would show up on a screen. Sometimes it's hard to believe that changing the way that you breathe works without your being attached to machines that measure your body response quantitatively.

Quantify your stress from one to ten. Write it down. Do your exercises and then reevaluate how you feel. You're probably going to go down one, two, or several points and feel better, and with practice you'll be able to do it faster each time.

THE SOLUTION

You don't have to take a meditation class in India or undergo long-term psychoanalytic therapy in order to learn to live in the now and be content. Short "active meditation" breathing techniques can lower your blood pressure, heart rate, and cortisol levels when practiced a few minutes a day. This daily "reboot" is exactly what you need. You don't need a vacation, you don't have to bear down and plow through work, day after day, without rest, until you get to your next vacation; you just need to *turn stress off* at regular intervals. You need to "turn off" so that your immune system can recharge—and you're about to learn how to do this in the next chapter.

My measure of my anxiety was when I could feel my heart beat. When I am about to have a panic attack, it rises to my throat and I have trouble focusing on anything else, and my vision for things far away and in the periphery gets short. My hands get cold and sweat. When all these come together, I know a full-blown panic attack is on the way. So I made that my measure: The next few times that happened, I put on my earphones and listened to the breath count. I timed how long it took me to feel my heart rate go back down. I realized that I had a moment of "turning the corner" when I would think, "I'm going to be okay," and the escalating would stop. For the next fourteen days, I practiced "bringing myself down"—it was fascinating to me that it worked every single time. Then it got to be how fast I could bring myself down. Now, when I get a hint of anxiety, I do a few deep LBB breaths to "reset" myself and keep moving. —Roxy, age 25

Apart from better breathing, this has changed my experience at boring meetings. Now instead of being stressed and irritated at the endless meetings, I do my breathing and Kegels and leave knowing I can check that off my list for the day. No one can see what I'm doing, and I just feel like I am multitasking my breathing workout for the day. Now I don't just sit there seething at all the dumb comments, I look interested but am really thinking, "inhale—expand," "exhale—squeeze." If they only knew! —Jessica, age 35

13

RECOVERY BREATH (AND MEDITATION FOR PEOPLE WHO CAN'T MEDITATE)

Recovery Breath is a form of active meditation and is completely different from any perception you may have of meditation. It's called "Recovery Breath" because it is a two-part breathing[63] exercise that helps reset your body after undergoing a grueling day at work, a disagreement with your spouse, a test or competition—any taxing or demanding situation.

If your usual routine during the week is to push hard and keep yourself going full speed until you get to the weekend, the best thing you can do is practice Recovery Breath five minutes a day. Yes, only five minutes a day! It won't make you groggy; in fact, if anything, it will refuel you. It will drench your body and every cell in it with oxygen, which is a big relief in view of the fact that your body has been running on unbalanced levels of carbon dioxide and low oxygen, adrenaline, and caffeine, due to your hectic schedule.

So, you may ask, after those five minutes, can I just hop back into my stressful existence and keep on going? Yes, indeed you can; but

---

63 I learned the two-part breath from author, teacher, and healer David Elliott. His website: http://www.davidelliott.com/.

you'll have increased mental clarity and more energy, and have the ability to problem-solve better and handle any irritability you may encounter during the day.

Long term, you'll protect yourself against high cortisol, heart disease, back problems, and migraines—and a host of diseases caused by chronic stress.

HEAR YOURSELF THINK

Your first question probably is, what specifically will this type of breathing/meditation do for me? I'll answer that succinctly. It will:

1. Quiet your mind so you can hear yourself think.
2. Let you distance yourself from your past, so that you can live more in the present. (This is what mindfulness is.)
3. Calm you to the point that you can hear your inner voice and be guided by your intuition.
4. Make you feel centered, balanced, and give you a distinct awareness of "your core."
5. Make you feel more connected to your own feelings, and to those of others.

Feel like shedding a tear, smiling, or laughing during this exercise? It is normal; that is the cathartic response. If this happens to you, don't repress the feeling. Let it out. Even if you don't know why it's happening, you'll undoubtedly feel lighter later on.

HOW LONG SHOULD I DO THE RECOVERY BREATH?

Initially, you will aim for two minutes; later you may graduate to three or four. To begin, set a gentle alarm to signal two minutes or find a song that you can have playing in the background for that time period. Since you are not doing this exercise with the guidance of a Breathwork practitioner, it should be gentler than the one you would do if you were in an actual class. Because breathing is both a conscious and unconscious process, it bridges both parts of your brain. Some people may have a cathartic response or release, and if they have suffered trauma in the past that they are now addressing, it is advisable to have someone to guide them through the exercise. However, if you are dealing with minimal routine stress and augment the time or difficulty of the two-part breath slowly each time you do it, there won't be an issue.

INSTRUCTIONS FOR THE RECOVERY BREATH: PART ONE

Start with the two-part breath, which is really two inhales. The first inhale fills your belly, the second, the top of your lungs. There's a very distinct division between the first and the second inhale, and each one should sound slightly different. The first one (which is an LBB) is fuller, as well.

1. Lying on your back, with nothing under your head, put one hand on your belly and one hand on the top of your chest, by your collarbones.

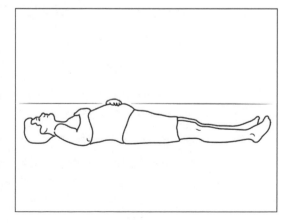

2. Breathe through your mouth. It is a bigger orifice than your nostrils, and the point of this exercise is to get more oxygen into your body and accustom yourself to breathing this way. It may feel peculiar at first, but you will get used to it after the second or third time.

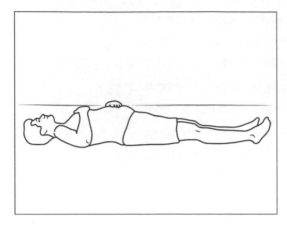

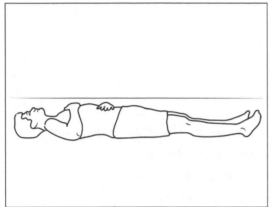

Your ego and your body may struggle with the newness of the Recovery Breath. Watch your reaction. Is it one of curiosity or irritation? Do you react negatively, get judgmental, or are you able to remain open-minded and gentle with your exercise?

3. The first inhale should make your belly rise; your top hand (on your chest) should not move. Now, without exhaling, take another inhale and fill the top of your lungs. This time, your top hand should move. To help you "learn" the breath, you can move your shoulders back slightly. *Be sure that you are not just transferring air from the bottom to the top.*

4. There should be two distinct inhales, even if the second one is small. It is not one long breath. Your belly should remain full as you add the second "top" breath. The first few times you inhale this way may feel odd. It should; you've never breathed like this before.

5. Exhale enthusiastically; it should take the amount of time the two inhales took, not longer. Exhale in one breath, feeling your chest and belly contract.

This first part in Recovery Breath should be hard; it is *exercise* for your breathing muscles. Note that the second inhale will feel smaller, even more constricted. You will probably feel pressure around your collarbones or armpits as you try to fill up this second breath. Some people even experience a "stitch" in their back as they try this new breathing, others a tightness in their necks. The general rule is to try to relax that place and continue inhaling.

There are three things to remember during part one of this exercise:

1. Keep breathing through your mouth for the entire first part. You may switch to your nose for the second part.
2. Find a rhythm that suits you, and stick to it. You should be able to find or "drop down" into this rhythm with more ease each time.
3. No matter what happens, just encourage yourself calmly and firmly to continue breathing. Any peculiar or uncomfortable sensations will lessen each time you practice, and the benefits are priceless.

Understand that you may hit a wall. Some people hit it after twenty breaths, others significantly later. In fact, the first few times you practice this active meditation you will hit the same kind of wall that you do when you work out. You will hear yourself make excuses about why you want to stop. Treat this feeling just as you do any other time you don't want to continue doing something but you have to. If you feel a little tingling, that's okay! Just encourage yourself to keep going, and remind yourself you are doing well and are almost done. Believe that there will be a moment when you get "to the other side," and just keep moving to the pace of your breath. It won't be like trudging uphill anymore.

INSTRUCTIONS FOR THE RECOVERY BREATH: PART TWO

Now you are going to switch to a big, gentle inhale and a big, gentle exhale.

1. Move your hands away from your body. Put your arms at your sides, palms up. Point your toes outward. You may keep breathing through your mouth or switch to your nose. Relax your lips, your face, your palate (the roof of your mouth). Let your tongue get heavy. Very important: Let your jaw relax. All of your body takes cues from your jaw. Pay attention to your cheeks, ears, and neck, relaxing them with each exhale. Relax your shoulders and your whole body—all the way to the tips of your fingers.

2. Continue doing mental body scans from time to time to make sure you are not holding tension anywhere. You may be surprised to discover that you may have a place that is always tensed, so much so that you have become accustomed to it. Be aware that with each inhale you are letting yourself float a little higher, and with each exhale you are letting yourself sink a little deeper. Try to move your mind away from thinking; simply keep your attention on your physical sensations. By "keep your attention on" I mean observe your body breathe as if you were watching another person.

Recovery Breath is pithy, involves active participation, and is immediately rewarding. It is a "two for the price of one" bargain: a brief but highly effective exercise that helps you recover from one day to the next, a form of active meditation for people who "can't meditate." Relaxing your body so that stress hormones and blood pressure decrease recharges your battery within minutes and encourages mindfulness. It protects you against the effects of prolonged stress by giving your body the oxygen and relaxation it needs to recover. In addition, Recovery Breath is a breathing exercise you can taper to meet your needs and level of enthusiasm.[64]

---

64 Are you liking the spiritual part of this more than you thought? Consider listening to Jack Kornfield's YouTube discussions or Dharma Punx's podcasts, or reading books by Pema Chodron or Thich Nhat Hanh from Sounds True, Inc.

In sum, Recovery Breath is a "reset" that will give your immune system a boost, keep your cortisol and blood pressure down, and oxygenate your body so that oxidative stress doesn't age you before your time. Do it as often as possible, ideally every day.

I immediately got light-headed as I did the two-part breath, but since I was lying down, all I had to do was remind myself that I couldn't fall, so it was safe. The feeling of newness was hard to deal with . . . as an adult, I almost never experience anything totally new where I have to trust that it is good for me (like when I was a kid). Though I would see myself hesitate, I just kept encouraging myself to continue. The first time was the hardest. After that, I think my breathing muscles got stronger and my understanding of the benefits outweighed my being skeptical and even a bit afraid. Afterward I felt lighter and recharged, like I'd taken a great nap. —Liz, age 65

Falling into a rhythm was what I focused on. I listened to my own breathing and just kept telling myself to keep with it, just as when I'm running. I hit a wall, but struggled through it and got a "second wind." It was oddly difficult, given that I was lying on my back. For part of the time, I was just confused as to why it was so hard. I had to shut out the talk in my head that wanted me to stop. I just told myself that I had nothing to lose, and that it wasn't frightening . . . it was interesting. Knowing that I was super-oxygenating my body and working out my breathing muscles made it easier to push through that hard moment, and though the subsequent times I practiced it was still work, it wasn't as hard as the first time. —Sean, age 32

Tracey's Story

A petite, feisty, twenty-nine-year-old spin instructor with an if-it-doesn't-kill-me-it-makes-me-stronger attitude, Tracey was the consummate calorie-burning cheerleader. She prided herself on having followers who attended her classes religiously, and she made one wonder if she ever napped or binged on ice cream like normal people. Despite knowing her cardio was excellent, she felt as if she couldn't get a big, satisfying, deep breath; in addition, after two years of leading spin classes, her voice was starting to become strained and raspy. Her ENT doctor told her she was at risk for throat nodules due to the strain on her voice her job required. Tracey panicked, googling "throat nodules" and "voice strain," which led to disturbing images of red, saliva-covered blisters and polyps. Then she found The Breathing Class, and having read testimonials from endurance athletes, she signed up. Spin instructors need the conditioning of triathletes *and* the vocal stamina of heavy metal singers. I discovered that while her cardio—the strength of her heart—was excellent, the sucking in of her waist (thinking this made her abs stronger), her tight workout clothes, and her habit of bracing her middle (a "readiness" stress stance) made Tracey's breathing mostly upper body; hence, she was breathing using her shoulders rather than her diaphragm. Her inhale was almost nonexistent, which made rapid, shallow breaths necessary. Tracey had to start with the very foundation: how and from where she inhaled and exhaled. "Letting her belly go" led to the beginnings of positive change; for her, the challenge was to be able to relax and stretch her middle (sides, back, and front). Three weeks later she was "out of the woods," feeling better; her throat healed, and she was able to take deep satisfying breaths.

14

BREATHING EXERCISES: THE BEST KEPT SECRET IN SPORTS—WHETHER YOU'RE A WEEKEND WARRIOR OR A PRO ATHLETE

You know the feeling of gasping for air. It happens when you just can't catch your breath, even if you're breathing as fast as you can. How often do you stop an exercise because you get winded? How often do you slow down because you feel as if you can't get enough oxygen? It's not due to your arms or legs giving out; it's literally a question of "catching your breath."[65] Specifically, *you can't get enough air in and out of your body fast enough to drive whatever you're doing.* So you stop.

So what if you *could* get enough air in and out fast enough?

The good news: you can—by strengthening the muscles that pull the air in and push it out of your body.

Doesn't regular exercise work out breathing muscles, too? No, it doesn't, and that's because you don't exercise the muscles to the point of exhaustion (when it gets to the point that your breathing muscles

---

65 "In fact the supply of oxygen becomes a secondary objective of breathing during heavy exercise, when the emphasis of its role switches to getting rid of the by-products of exercise, carbon dioxide" (Alison McConnell, *Breathe Strong, Perform Better*, p. 68).

are getting a workout, the rest of your muscles are already slowing down). You must work out breathing muscles *separately*.

If this is news to you, don't worry. Studies on breathing and breathing muscles in sports didn't start until the 1980s. Before then, it was simply assumed that the diaphragm adapted to continuous activity. But it doesn't, and this takes a big toll on your performance.

Take two athletes with the same amount of talent, heart, and strength. The one who'd followed a breathing-muscle workout will indubitably dominate.

FAQ: How much does my gene pool have to do with my breathing? While your heredity dictates the efficacy of pulmonary and tissue diffusion (the transfer of gas from air in the lungs to the red blood cells), you *can* make massive changes *in the strength of your breathing muscles*—the pump that makes oxygen available to your lungs.

BRING YOUR A-GAME

Breathing for Warriors is a class I teach for athletes who want better conditioning and endurance (think CrossFit or mixed martial arts—MMA). There are two major goals:

1. Adding oxygen to your blood. The common reaction to "gassing," or running out of breath, is, "I have to do more cardio." If the point of cardio is to improve the circulation of blood driven by your heart in order to get more oxygen to your body, then why not consider adding more oxygen to your blood, instead? It makes sense, right?

   Action: Making sure every breath you take is an efficacious

Why is breathing from the biggest part of your lungs and making sure your breathing muscles are in shape so important? The average adult breathes ten to fifteen times per minute, but during exercise up to *five times as much*—a whopping forty to fifty times.

one. Breathing mechanics *take up energy,* so why not make each breath you take the biggest one possible?

2. Incorporating a breathing workout. Much of the fatigue experienced during exercise comes from the *breathing* muscles getting tired.

Action: Unless you have a specific breathing workout (which often means the rest of your body is *not* moving), you're not working out your breathing muscles in a way that makes them stronger.

The breathing workout and drills you're practicing with this book will:

1. Give you endurance and conditioning past what any cardio workout could do on its own. Pick a measure of your endurance now, and watch how it changes as you do your breathing workout over the next few weeks. You'll find that the point at which you tire gets later, and that your scores or times improve.[66]

2. Increase the speed at which you heal, due to oxygenation of muscles, and protect yourself against falling into a depression (caused in part by lack of endorphins). For athletes, injuries are a fate worse than death: your plans change, you can't move, you feel as if you're losing all the gains you've made. Having a breathing workout means that, despite an immobilizing injury, you can still sweat

---

66 For a detailed study on this subject, see Craig A. Harms et al., "Effects of Respiratory Muscle Work on Exercise Performance," *Journal of Applied Physiology* 89, no. 1 (2000): 1131–38.

and work out *on the inside*. These exercises raise your levels of endorphins and healing oxygen, despite that ACL tear or fracture.

3. Give you nerves of steel. Upper-body Breathing automatically makes you anxious; Horizontal Breathing helps get you in the "zone" and stay there. You'll have the ability to withstand more discomfort and push past the pain threshold that could otherwise hold you back. You'll eliminate perplexing gassing on the court or playing field because you will have gained *balanced energy that comes with better breathing.*

> FAQ: *So even though I run until I am breathing so hard that I have to stop, this isn't working out my breathing muscles? It sure feels like it.* In order to strengthen any muscle, you have to push it past exhaustion, and to do this, you have to work out your breathing muscles on their own. What does that mean? Do Exhale Pulsations and Recovery Breath until you sweat. The harder you work out your inhale and exhale, the less you will tire when you are practicing or competing.

> FAQ: *Why do I get so panicky before a race? I've been practicing positive affirmations, but they don't seem to work.* The anxiety that comes with competition usually depends on what is at stake (be it purse or pride). Your breathing responds to what is on the line; consequently, the way in which you breathe can make you more anxious. Once you get your breathing under control, your neurology automatically goes along with it and your mantras and positive self-talk will work much better.

Let's talk about three topics critical to your success that are intimately involved in your breathing: *Recovery, your "inner game," and how to breathe when you lift and run.*

RECOVERY—ALL YOU NEED IS TEN MINUTES A DAY

One of the most important and most overlooked aspects of training is *recovery*. If you don't give yourself time to recover between workouts, you put yourself at risk for injury and will plateau as far as learning and getting stronger are concerned. But taking a long weekend off may be out of the question, plus during downtime, what your brain finds relaxing—video games, Facebook, TV—may not really be helping your body. So how do you "relax fast"? The meditation exercise you learned in the last chapter is called Recovery Breath; however, when I teach it to athletes, it's about oxygenating, lowering cortisol, healing, and pushing that reset button so they can train again effectively tomorrow.

YOUR INNER GAME: HOW TO KEEP A COOL HEAD AND STAY BALANCED

Whether it's a jolt of happiness as the ball makes it in, or literally a kick in the head from an opponent, bursts of energy can be extreme and can negatively affect your judgment if not controlled. "Bad" breathing can exacerbate this. Breathing, then, is the ultimate way to keep that adrenaline in balance: you want to be *calm and alert*.[67] Unfortunately, fluctuations in energy and emotion can become a potentially dangerous enemy, hurting your peripheral vision and warping your time perception.

---

67 Cesar Millan, the "Dog Whisperer," constantly tells dog owners to stay calm and assertive. On an episode that aired on March 18 this year, I taught an anxious dog owner to breathe in a "calm but assertive" way.

DO THIS

Practice adversity. Yes, practice; don't assume that you'll know what to do when you need to calm yourself quickly. In my Breathing for Warriors class, I make participants practice getting revved up and then calming down, until it becomes a mastered skill.[68]

In both competition and in occupational situations, it can be very tough to calm down after you've experienced a major energy surge. The rush keeps you vibrating and on edge, even when you want to calm down. Instead, you're still buzzing but sapped of energy. Modulating your energy levels and not letting nerves tap into your reserves of energy is a challenge every athlete faces. The knowledge about the subtleties of your body and your own mind that breathing will teach you will definitely give you a better grasp of cellular metabolism and put you in control of your own gas tank. It's a state of mind that comes naturally to very few. The good news is that it is a state of mind that can be achieved by practicing breathing that calms you.

FAQ: You talk about efficient breath; why is that so important? If you are taking dramatic Vertical Breaths—moving your upper body and shoulders instead of using your diaphragm—you are using up a lot of energy (which is called "the mechanical cost of lung expansion"). A more efficient Lower-body Breath accesses the biggest, most oxygen-dense part of your lungs, with muscles that use up less energy.

FAQ: So if I breathe better, I'll have more energy? Yes, because cellular metabolism—reactions in the cell that produce energy—is regulated by the oxygen provided during breathing.

---

68 Big wave surfer and waterman Laird Hamilton is a strong proponent of "having a good relationship with your breath" as a way to control anxiety. Take a look online at his underwater workouts if you're tired of working out on land.

Your "inner game" is the ease with which you get "into the zone" and find your tempo, your rhythm . . . It all has to do with your breath, but you have to study it pragmatically, as you're doing now.

Deep breathing after exercise is important since *post-exercise oxygen consumption* (PEOC) often occurs. Basically, your metabolism stays elevated, and your body continues using up more oxygen than normal for several hours. Getting extra oxygen is a good thing, as it'll decrease this oxygen deficit.

If you're a surfer and getting hit by that second (or third) wave, you better make sure you have a good breath-hold. In my advanced classes, I include exercises on retention that are very important both for breath-holds and for mental toughness, as well.[69]

There are moments when holding your breath is good.[70] (In fact, there's a split second at the bottom of your exhale when you are most at peace, most still.) At the end of an exhale, if you're putting in golf or shooting at a range, you need your most steady heartbeat.

FAQ: Do I mess up my energy if I hold my breath? Yes, because when you stop breathing, you throw your body and brain into a complete imbalance from which it's very difficult to recover quickly. It can take a while for your body to recalibrate its levels of oxygen and carbon dioxide. Holding your breath (as when you're anxious) reduces beneficial antioxidants in the body.

---

69 However, given that breath-holding as a dysfunctional breathing style ("e-mail apnea") is epidemic nowadays, for beginners I focus on the importance of keeping their breath fluid and balanced/ongoing.

70 During a workshop I conducted for the DEA in San Diego, an agent described his breath-hold as being necessary when going into a dangerous situation. Breathing can obstruct the ability to hear subtle movements when entering a silent room.

Remember, the biggest mistake you can make if you're doing a sport is to hold your breath too long.[71]

A study in the *Journal of Applied Physiology* demonstrates the significant effect of "the work of breathing" during strenuous exercise on performance time to exhaustion in healthy, physically trained humans. Craig A. Harms et al. observed that increasing the effectiveness of breathing consistently led to significantly longer exercise tolerance; increasing "the work of breathing" curtailed performance. Their findings demonstrate that "the work of breathing" normally encountered during sustained heavy exercise has an impact on exercise performance.

BREATHING WHEN LIFTING AND RUNNING

Lifting—three points to keep in mind to do it right:

1. Inhale with a big belly breath (relaxing your hips/glutes), then contract your middle before lifting in order to create intrathoracic pressure. Contracting will help *brace the load* during heavier lifts while maintaining lumbar stability.[72]

2. Exhale *on the exertion*. Using the bench press as an example, exhale slowly and continuously while pressing the bar. While you may have to hold the breath momentarily past the "sticking" point, make sure you go back to exhaling immediately afterward. (If the movement is a fast one, like a strike or a punch, the goal should be a *forced* exhalation.)

3. A little known fact is that you need to protect your pelvic floor when lifting, otherwise you'll end up with pelvic-floor herniation

---

71 Another way of saying that anxiety breath-holding spells are bad not only for you but others around you is often heard in the equine world, from a trainer to a rider: "Stop holding your breath—you are scaring the horse."

72 What is better: hollowing or bracing? Bracing is the right way. For more on this, go to www.t-nation.com/training/freakish-strength-with-proper-core -training.

(think leaking when you cough or laugh) over time. During the inhale, relax your body, *then* contract the pelvic floor, *then* contract the abs to stabilize the spine. *Go!*

Running—three points to keep in mind to do it right:

1. Breathing low will help your center of gravity while running. Vertical Breathing actually puts your center of gravity a foot higher, which is unbalancing.
2. Breathing low also means a more efficient breath, using less energy and creating more. A bigger breath means you have more flexibility to regulate your breathing to match your stride. Budd Coates is the expert when it comes to rhythmic running.[73]
3. Lower-body Breaths calm the system, so you can get "in the zone" when running faster. Note: Synchronizing your breath to your running cadence will keep the organs from putting unnecessary pressure on the diaphragm.

When the cardiovascular system can keep up with the demands of an exercise, the exercise is said to be "aerobic"; but when the demands of the exercise exceed our cardiovascular capacity, the exercise is considered "anaerobic." Once the accumulated toxins in your body reach a certain point, you "hit the wall." Anaerobic exercise is especially beneficial in that it increases the capacity of the cardiovascular system. The good news is that breathing exercises also help raise that capacity.

ANAEROBIC EXERCISE

Anaerobic exercise differs from aerobic in its use of oxygen. While aerobic exercise develops a continual process of energy delivery by continual oxygen use, anaerobic exercise allows the body to function on pre-prepared energy stored directly in the cell itself. This energy is

---

73 Check out his book *Running on Air*.

generally accessed when the body is pushed to more than 90 percent of its typical physical output. Typical training of the anaerobic system usually involves intervals or circuits which push the body to total output for a short period of time, ranging from a few seconds to around four minutes at the higher end.

FAQ: What happens when I "get the wind knocked out of me"? What can I do about it? You can get the wind knocked out of you if you're thrown unexpectedly in judo, or if you hit the ground jarringly as when falling from a horse. What you experience is essentially a diaphragm spasm. You can do several things: cough or pretend to laugh (although this is probably really the last thing on your mind), or push your belly out hard to inhale, then push your sides together to exhale. Think of it exactly like a knot or spasm in any muscle. Much of the jolt comes with the psychological surprise of being "thrown," and the antidote is to practice falling so that when it happens you know exactly how to react.

FAQ: Isn't my breathing automatically better because I do yoga? No, not all yoga improves breathing. I find that often people in class are ignoring the instructions to "inhale, two, three, four, exhale, two, three, four," and instead are holding their breath during difficult poses. In addition, some hot or power yoga propels you into dysfunctional

High-Altitude Training

The fundamental theory of altitude training proposes that by exposing athletes to an environment that is low in oxygen, their bodies adapt to the stress by improving their oxygen intake efficiency, thereby enhancing physical performance. According to this theory, if athletes can adjust their bodies to perform at competitive levels with less oxygen in their blood and muscles, then while competing at sea level, they should have higher endurance levels. Unfortunately, research hasn't documented much consistent value in high-altitude training.

upper-body panting and breath-holding. Looking for something to help you breathe? I suggest qigong, in which at least the pacing and movement are synchronized; if you're able to keep your breathing low at your belly, you'll be golden.

THE GAME-CHANGING FIVE

There are five basic exercises that athletes learn to perfection when working with me.

1. Exhale when exerting energy.[74] The exhale will help strengthen whatever you're propelling, be it a fist or a baseball, or a weight when bench-pressing.

   Homework: You may think you're exhaling, but check how often you're really holding your breath. Practice integrating the breath into movement—this will help with the strength of the movement and its fluidity.

2. Face your enemies. Your worst enemy is "perceived fatigue." Crushing this opponent is possible by working out your breathing muscles diligently.

   Homework: How often do you wonder why you're lacking focus, energy, or motivation? Check yourself. It may be your breathing is off (rather than your being lazy or lacking passion).

3. Breathe horizontally. Your second-worst enemy is adrenaline or an erratic amount of "gas." Breathing vertically causes this.

---

74 The gym grunt has a purpose (unless it's an overly dramatic attention-seeking grunt). This same grunt is *essential* in tennis and at the apex of a sharp turn in skiing. We also hear a version of it in ancient martial arts, *precipitating* contact, in an effort to have the breath "guide" and reinforce the force.

(Remember: Oxygen is used by the cells to release energy from the body's energy stores.)

Homework: Check your shoulders. Sure, on a bigger breath, there's going to be some movement; however, your shoulders shouldn't be your inhale muscles exclusively. Consciously taking a Lower-body Breath is giving you a significantly bigger breath, and neurologically, a calming one.

4. Exhale: Troubleshoot hyperventilating. All too often, people brace when they're in competitive situations, which can lead to over-breathing/hyperventilating afterward.

Homework: Rather than tell yourself to "breathe," say, "exhale."

5. If your sport relies on precision, learn to recognize and expand the stillness in the last second of the exhale. In precision sports like archery, golf, or shooting, if you don't replicate the breath exactly with your "pre-shot routine," you're leaving a big factor to chance, which can make for infuriating inconsistencies.

Homework: When doing the Recovery Breathing meditation, bring attention to the stillness that you feel between breaths.

Before my tournament, I do some of the breathing skills Dr. Belisa taught me, and it puts me in a perfect mental state to dismantle my competition. After she started working with me, as a brown belt I fought seven matches in the NAGA No-Gi Expert division without breaking a sweat or having my guard passed even once. I used my breathing techniques anytime I was in a tight position. The breathing exercises that Dr. Belisa taught me were able to put me into a mental state that allowed me to have incredible endurance. —Mike, age 27

EPILOGUE

Sometimes a change in your life sends out ripples in unexpected directions. I do hope that this will be your experience with *Breathe*: that it will pique your curiosity about other types of exercises and topics related to breathing. You might be moved to explore different patterns of breathing from such experts as Dr. Andrew Weil, Dr. Richard Brown, and Dr. Patricia Gerbarg. You might even try Water Breathing with Dr. Jim Morningstar; deepen your understanding of yoga breathing[75] with Leslie Kaminoff; take a meditation class with Gabby Bernstein; refine your knowledge of anatomy by studying Blandine Calais-Germain's beautiful illustrations in *Anatomy of Breathing*; do a workshop with David Elliott; learn Kriya Breathing at The Art of Living; or pore over Patrick McKeown, or Al Lee and Don Campbell's *Perfect Breathing*.

I hope you'll be moved to read the works of visionaries and researchers whose passion has been to teach and study breathing: psychiatrist and researcher "Stan" (Stanislav) Grof, Dr. Leon Chaitow, Dr. Gay Hendricks, and Donna Farhi, to name just a few. You might listen with new interest to Joe Rogan's podcasts in which he talks about breathing, or read up on the adventures of free divers Stig Sev-

---

75 For a beautiful summary of how breath is considered the cornerstone of health, see *Science of Breath* by Yogi Ramacharaka, Appendix 2.

erinsen and Natalia Avseenko. Maybe you'll feel so impassioned you'll take a specialized Kundalini yoga class or join the virtual breathing space Do As One (Doasone.com).

Maybe, just maybe, you'll assimilate this information and be inspired to help your loved ones and talk to them about their breath, their lungs, their breathing muscles. I'll finish this book the same way I bring to a close Recovery Breath/Meditation: by asking you to "bring a small smile to your face and let it flow through your entire body. This is a smile of gratitude, giving thanks for *everything* that you are and *everything* that you have, for all the love that is around you and all the love that is within you. But most of all, giving thanks to yourself for having made the time to take care of your body, your mind, and your soul."

TAKEAWAY POINTS

- Having an imbalance of oxygen and carbon dioxide can create serious problems related to inflammation and acidity, but without delving into the chemistry, simply know that you need to pay attention to both.
- The harder you work out your inhale and exhale, the less you'll tire when you're practicing or competing.
- Stress in the body raises cortisol in the muscles, and therefore places strain on the back through excess diaphragm tension. What this means is that negative emotions (e.g., sadness, anger) hurt your back.
- Better inhales and exhales are part of the solution; addressing stress levels (and even deeper, subconscious emotional pain) is a big part of the cure.
- Vertical Breathing means you're overusing neck and shoulder muscles (at the front *and* back of your body), which then throws the balance of muscles off all the way down your body. And it really does throw your balance off. Your natural center of gravity is right below your belly button. So you aren't imagining the feeling of being more balanced when you breathe low; it's real. As your center of gravity gets lower, you become both physically and emotionally more balanced.

- On the inhale, you should be thinking two things: Lower-body Breath and expand. On the exhale, think: Lower-body Breath and squeeze/contract. Remind yourself: "Inhale . . . expand. Exhale . . . squeeze."

- Between each breath, a certain amount of carbon dioxide stays in your lungs, just settling there and getting stale (more if you are a really lazy exhaler). The result is that these organs can't expand to their full capacity with fresh air on your next inhalation. In other words, your starting inhalations *have* to be less than optimal when you haven't exhaled well. Often, the result is that you speed up the rate of your breathing in an effort to compensate, which ripples out as an imbalance of pretty much everything in your body and nervous system.

- Lower-body Breathing is anatomically congruous; Vertical Breathing is not—you're going against the way your body and organs were built. A Lower-body Breath that expands on the inhale is a healthy breath. Turn your awareness inward: You'll find it "feels good." You're not imagining it.

FAQ: How was I exhaling before? Before, you were using your shoulders to exhale: letting them fall and relaxing your belly—a very, very ineffective way to exhale.

- The belly breath really is just the beginner breath that helps break down the habit of keeping the middle of your body braced. It gets you physically used to the idea that there is movement from your armpits to your pelvis when you breathe.

FAQ: You talk about activating the diaphragm; when did it deactivate? It started when you started bracing your body, either as an emotional response or when sucking in your gut because you thought it was good for you. Little by little, your diaphragm got replaced by your neck and shoulder muscles, which would pull you up to breathe. Not to worry, though, because gaining understanding, stretching, and practicing the exercises in this book will get it back in gear, no matter how old you are now.

- The next stage in maximizing your inhalations is to consider the flexibility of your thoracic cavity. If you sit at a desk at work or spend several hours a day in a car, then your thoracic cavity is probably pretty darn rigid—the size of your lungs doesn't matter. Making the intercostal muscles (between your ribs, and in your sides and back) more flexible means they'll expand more, allowing you to take a bigger breath.

- At the top of your breath (and remember you aren't really filling *up*—you are filling *out*), relax your shoulders again and let the air feel as if it's settling into your body. Then soften your pelvis (meaning relax your glutes and thighs) and notice the feeling of being more grounded. This should only take two to three seconds.

- At this point, you should be able to imagine in your mind's eye how your pelvic diaphragm is the "bottom" of a container. Your belly and upper abs are the middle of the container, and your thoracic diaphragm is at the top. Some people envision a poster tube, others a long water balloon.

GLOSSARY OF TYPES OF BREATHING

This list is not exhaustive; these are breathing exercises and methods that you may want to research and consider now that you have a good foundation for basic breathing.

(THE) 4-7-8 BREATHING EXERCISE: An example of a Counting Breath or Breathing Isometric, in this technique one inhales quietly through the nose and exhales audibly through the mouth. The tip of your tongue is placed against the ridge of tissue just behind the upper front teeth through the entire exercise. The inhale is through the nose for 4 counts, breath is held for 7, the exhale is completely through your mouth, making a *whoosh* sound for 8. The cycle is repeated 3 more times.

BELLY BREATHING: Also known as "Abdominal" Breathing, it's marked by expansion of the abdomen, rather than the upper chest. While the belly breathing taught in this book is exaggerated and important for dismantling bad breathing habits, a slight expansion of the middle is important in that it means the diaphragm is moving to expand the middle, where the best part of the lungs are pushing abdominal organs down (which helps with digestion) to create more room in the rib cage for the lungs to expand to their capacity.

BREATHWALK: Combines distinct patterns of breathing—ratios, intervals, and breath types—that are synchronized with walking steps and meditative attention. Directed breathing and focused attention can be utilized for personal growth, to control pain, and to induce relaxation, and are used in many forms of martial arts and athletics.

BUDDHIST BREATHING: Buddha quite openly and continually advocated Breath Meditation or *Anapanasati*, an awareness of the inhaling and exhaling breaths. It starts with an awareness of the ordinary physical breath, which, when cultivated correctly, leads one into higher awareness.

BUTEYKO BREATHING: Based on the assumption that numerous medical conditions, especially asthma, are caused by hyperventilation, this breathing technique (breathing slowly through the nose) was developed in the 1950s by Konstantin Buteyko, a Ukrainian doctor. It purports to break the vicious cycle of rapid, gasping breaths, airway constriction, and wheezing.

CIRCULAR BREATH: Produces a continuous tone, often used by players of wind instruments. By breathing *in* through the nose while simultaneously pushing air *out* through the mouth using air stored in the cheeks, an uninterrupted tone is achieved. It is used extensively in playing many instruments; e.g., the Australian didgeridoo, the Sardinian *launeddas*, and the Egyptian *arghul*. A few jazz and classical wind and brass players also utilize some form of Circular Breathing. Essentially, Circular Breathing bridges the gap between exhalations. The air stored in the person's cheeks is used as an extra air reserve to play with while they sneak in a breath through their nose. Bounce Breathing is an advanced form of Circular Breathing.

CLAVICULAR BREATHING (aka Shallow Breathing): Clavicle Breathing draws air into the chest area by the raising of the shoulders and collarbone (clavicles). Oxygen reaches only the top third of the lungs; this is the most superficial mode of Shallow Breathing. *See also Costal Breathing, below.*

COHERENT BREATHING: Involves breathing at the nominal rate of five breaths per minute with an equal inhalation and exhalation. This method claims to facilitate circulation and autonomic nervous system balance by creating a wave in the circulatory system, the "Valsalva Wave" (a term coined by Stephen Elliott).

COSTAL BREATHING (aka Lateral Breathing): A technique in which inspiration and expiration are produced chiefly by horizontal/lateral movements of the ribs.

COUNTING BREATH (BREATHING ISOMETRICS): With the body re-laxed, a breathing pattern is maintained. Depth and rhythm may vary. Inhales should last several seconds; exhales are long and slow through your teeth, or with pursed lips, whichever feels more comfortable. When in an isometric exercise position, a regular count should be established, because holding the breath during exercise is not a good idea—and may even be dangerous.

DIAPHRAGMATIC BREATHING: A type of breathing exercise that promotes more effective aeration of the lungs, consisting of moving the diaphragm downward during inhalation and upward during exhalation.

HOLOTROPIC BREATHING: Developed by Stanislav Grof as an approach to self-exploration and healing that integrates insights from Eastern spiritual practices as well as modern consciousness research in transpersonal psychology. The method comprises five components: group process, intensified breathing, evocative music, focused body-work, and expressive drawing.

LATERAL BREATHING: Focuses on filling your sides and back. The exhale brings the entire middle into the center. It's sometimes used interchangeably with Costal Breathing, which is used to deepen the voice and to treat stammering; however, in Costal Breathing the focus is on the rib cage all the way around the body.

LUNG CAPACITY: There are two different measures of lung breathing capacity: Tidal Volume, which is the amount of air that flows in and out of your lungs during normal breathing; and Vital Lung Capacity, which is the maximum amount of air that can move in and out of your lungs. Tidal Volume is the breathing you do without thinking. Vital Lung Capacity is the equivalent of taking a deep breath before going under water or exhaling fully after surfacing. In a clinical setting, doctors measure Vital Lung Capacity with a device called a "spirometer."

MERKABA BREATHING: A meditation that consists of seventeen breaths, each visualized as a different geometric shape. It's based on the theory that the physical body and spirit can be transported through different dimensions. Also called "Spherical Breathing."

NADI SHODHANA PRANAYAMA (aka "alternate nostril breathing"): Used to destress, relax, and balance the mind. To complete the first round, press the thumb on the right nostril and breathe out gently through the left nostril. Next breathe in through the left nostril gently, then press closed with the ring finger. Remove the thumb from the right nostril and breathe out through the right nostril. Breathe in through the right nostril, close, and exhale from the left. Continue with the inhales and exhales, alternating between nostrils.

PATTERNED BREATHING: Uses a certain "count" for the inhale and the exhale. Some have "holds" or "retention" at the top of the inhale or top of the exhale, while in others the exhale starts immediately after the inhale is full. The goal of patterned breathing is to slow down the breath and either distract (from pain) or help focus on the breath.

PERFECT BREATHING: Promotes slower breath and fosters an alert state of mind and a relaxed breathing. The technique is to be used several times a day and should show immediate benefits. Don Campbell, proponent of the method, reports improved mental focus and increased energy. Related practices include: Energy Wave Breathing, Waterfall Breathing, and Imagination Breathing. Also termed "Conscious Breathing."

PRANAYAMA BREATH: Yogic breathing techniques that help control the *"prana"* or vital life force (also known as "chi," "qi," or "ki"). The most popular are *Dirga Pranayama* (Three-part Breath), *Ujjayi Pranayama,* (Ocean Breath), *Nadi Shodhana Pranayama* (alternate nostril breathing), and *Kapalabhati Pranayama* (Light Skull Breathing).

PRANIC BREATHING: A six-step form of breathing that aspires to increase, control, and direct the *prana,* or vital life force. The first step clears negative emotions and limiting beliefs; the second utilizes a highly energizing breathing technique to boost vitality; the third manipulates energy (through scanning, sweeping, and energizing); the fourth step involves energetic hygiene; the fifth step, meditation; the sixth and final step consists of the two very powerful energy-generation exercises.

RECOVERY BREATH: A fast breathing exercise that is a combination of all the preliminary exercises taught, that then goes into a state of gentle "natural" breathing, rest, and a meditative state. It helps to calm and recover after a competition or test. Calming the body, lowering cortisol, and going back to a "rest and digest" alert but calm state helps combat the effects of oxidative stress. Recovery Breath is also called "Active Meditation."

REICHIAN BREATHING (ARMOR): Wilhelm Reich related difficulties in emotional well-being to functional problems on a bodily level, as reflected in disturbed breathing. He induced a sense of peace and calm in his patients by guiding them to focus only on their breath. In Reich's opinion, the blocking of feeling, motility, and energy in the body creates an "armor" that defends one from threatening internal impulses and from external dangers.

RESISTANCE BREATHING: The goal is to employ resistance in order to strengthen the muscles used in respiration. Apart from people with breathing disorders, many singers, divers, martial arts practitioners, and athletes incorporate resistance breathing into their regimen. Resistance may be provided with the use of respiratory muscle trainers, or by creating physical obstacles—such as pursing the lips to increase resistance during breathing.

RHYTHMIC BREATHING: A breathing technique used for running described by Budd Coates in his book *Runner's World Running on Air*. It centers around the idea that rhythmic breathing increases lung volume; improves awareness and control; helps prevent injury and side stitches; improves running for those with asthma; allows runners to quickly set a pace for quality training and racing; and helps athletes manage muscle cramps.

SITHALI: Referred to as "tongue hissing" because during the inhale, air is drawn in through a protruding tongue folded into a tube. As a result, the air passes over a moist tongue, thereby refreshing the throat. Faster or slower inhalation makes possible variations in the loudness and softness and smoothness of a reversed hissing sound. The tongue is drawn back into the mouth, and the lips are closed at the end of inhalation. One can breathe out either through the mouth or alternately through the nostrils.

SPORTS BREATHING: Breathing techniques related to improved performance during such sports as swimming, biking, or weight lifting, or breathing exercises for endurance and conditioning that train inspiratory and expiratory breathing muscles. Also used after competitive events to reduce stress and tension and induce a calmer state.

TAO YIN BREATHING: Consists of postures, meditation, and breathing patterns to strengthen and relax the back and energize and relax the lumbar area. The goal, explains Taoist Master Mantak Chia, is to achieve harmony between chi and external energies, and revitalize the body and spirit. Also known as Taoist Yoga.

TAOIST REVERSE BREATHING: Traditionally used by qigong practitioners, healers, and martial artists, it reverses the in-and-out movements of the abdomen present in natural breathing: the abdomen contracts inward during inhalation and relaxes outward during exhalation. When the diaphragm moves downward and the belly contracts inward during inhalation, the resulting pressure in the abdomen "packs" the breath energy; when the diaphragm relaxes upward and the belly relaxes outward during exhalation, the pressure is suddenly released. Taoist Reverse Breathing is an advanced technique and should only be undertaken with guidance.

THORACIC BREATHING: A dysfunctional, ineffective way of breathing that does not use the diaphragm, but rather the intercostal muscles. Thoracic breathing tends to be inefficient, shallow, and rapid, which may result in too much carbon dioxide retained in the body and respiratory acidosis.

TRANSFORMATIONAL BREATHING: Popularized by Dr. Judith Kravitz, who posits that this technique facilitates the natural healing process for all types of trauma and for beneficial maintenance of optimal health, Transformational Breathing is an active exercise that uses the breath to release tension within the body. The breathing technique is a deep breath in through the mouth while inflating the abdomen and a gentle sigh out on the exhale. There is no pause between inhale and exhale.

YOGIC BREATH: Incorporates three types of breathing—Collarbone (Clavicular) Breathing, Chest Breathing, and Abdominal or Diaphragmatic Breathing—thereby utilizing full lung capacity. With the inhalation, the abdomen extends forward and the chest is expanded; with the exhalation, the chest and the abdomen return to their original position, united into a flowing wave.

APPENDIX 1: MEASURES

There are numerous other measures you can use in order to determine the state of your breathing. The following are done at your doctor's office:

1. Bloodwork CO_2: Usually conducted during a standard electrolyte or metabolic panel, this test measures the amount of bicarbonate (HCO3-) in the blood. Results indicating an imbalance of oxygen and carbon dioxide may suggest kidney or lung dysfunction.

2. Spirometry (e.g., FVC and FEV1): A fairly common lung function test, spirometry measures the amount of air that can be exhaled after a full inhalation. Forced vital capacity (FVC) refers to the total amount of expelled air after a forcible exhalation, while forced expiratory volume in one second (FEV1) refers to the total amount of air exhaled in the first second. Results of this test may indicate a range of lung dysfunctions.

3. VO_2 Max: This refers to the maximum rate of oxygen consumption during aerobic exercise. Measuring VO_2 max typically involves a graded exercise test on a treadmill or stationary bicycle, in which ventilation and O_2 and CO_2 concentration are recorded while the exercise increases in intensity. VO_2 max determines physical fitness and endurance.

4. A test of your heart rate variability: Heart rate variability refers to the difference in time between heartbeats. Increased heart rate variability reflects good cardiovascular health, for it implies that the heart is responsive to the body's demands. However, decreased variability may correlate to poorer cardiovascular health, and recent studies suggest that it might impact the prognosis of patients with myocardial infarction and chronic heart failure.

On your own, you can take the following measurements:

1. Use a finger pulse oximeter (most drugstores carry them).
2. Observe the rate of your breath (the general rule is that slower is better).
3. Take a one-time breath-hold (the average is forty-five seconds).
4. Measure your own acidity (pH strips).
5. Note your resting heart rate.

APPENDIX 2: SCIENCE OF BREATH

PHYSIOLOGICAL EFFECT OF THE COMPLETE BREATH

Too much can't be said about the advantages attending the practice of the Complete Breath. And yet, the student who has carefully read the foregoing pages should scarcely need to have pointed out to him such advantages.

The practice of the Complete Breath will make any man or woman immune to consumption and other pulmonary troubles, and will do away with all likelihood of contracting "colds," as well as bronchial and similar weaknesses. Consumption is principally due to lowered vitality, attributable to an insufficient amount of air being inhaled. The impairment of vitality renders the system open to attacks from disease germs. Imperfect breathing allows a considerable part of the lungs to remain inactive, and such portions offer an inviting field for bacilli which, invading the weakened tissue, soon produce havoc. Good, healthy lung tissue will resist the germs, and the only way to have good healthy lung tissue is to use the lungs properly.

Consumptives are nearly all narrow-chested. What does this mean? Simply that these people are addicted to improper habits of breathing, and consequently their chests failed to develop and expand. The man who practices the Complete Breath will have a full, broad chest, and the narrow-chested man may develop his chest to normal proportions if he will but adopt this mode of breathing. Such people must develop their chest cavities if they value their lives. Colds may often be prevented by practicing a little vigorous Complete Breathing whenever you feel that you are being unduly exposed. When chilled, breathe vigorously a few minutes, and you'll feel a glow all over your body. Most colds can be cured by Complete Breathing and partial fasting for a day.

The quality of the blood depends largely upon its proper oxygenation in the lungs; if under-oxygenated, it becomes poor in quality and laden with all sorts of impurities, and the system suffers from a lack of nourishment, and often becomes actually poisoned by the waste products remaining in the blood. As the entire body, every organ and every part, is dependent upon the blood for nourishment, impure blood must have a serious effect upon the entire system. The remedy is plain—practice the Yogi Complete Breath.

The stomach and other organs of nutrition suffer greatly from improper breathing. Not only are they ill nourished by a lack of oxygen, but as the food must absorb oxygen from the blood and become oxygenated before it can be digested and assimilated, it's easy to see how digestion and assimilation are impaired by incorrect breathing. And when assimilation is abnormal, the system receives less and less nourishment, the appetite fails, bodily vigor decreases, energy diminishes, and the body withers and declines—all from a lack of proper breathing.

Even the nervous system suffers from improper breathing, inasmuch as the brain, the spinal cord, the nerve centers, and the nerves themselves, when improperly nourished by means of the blood, become poor and inefficient instruments for generating, storing, and transmitting the nerve currents. And if sufficient oxygen is not absorbed through the lungs, they'll become improperly nourished. There is another aspect of the case whereby the nerve currents themselves, or rather the force from which the nerve currents spring, becomes lessened from want of proper breathing, but this belongs to another phase of the subject, which is treated in other chapters of this book; our purpose here is to direct your attention to the fact that the mechanism of the nervous system is rendered inefficient as an instrument for conveying nerve force as the indirect result of a lack of proper breathing.

The effect of the reproductive organs upon the body's general health is too well known to be discussed at length here, but we will say that, with the reproductive organs in a weakened condition, the entire system feels the reflex action and suffers sympathetically. The Complete Breath produces a rhythm which is Nature's own plan for keeping this important part of the system in normal condition, and, from the first, you'll notice that the reproductive functions are strengthened and vitalized, thus, by sympathetic reflex action, giving tone to your whole bodily system. By this, we do not mean that the lower sex impulses will be aroused; far from it. Yogis are actually advocates of continence and chastity, and have learned to control the "animal passions." But sexual control does not mean sexual weakness, and the Yogic teachings state that the man or woman whose reproductive organs are normal and healthy will have a stronger will with which to control him- or herself. The Yogi believes that much of the perversion of this wonderful part of the system comes from a lack of normal health, and results from a morbid rather than a normal condition of these organs. A little careful consideration of this question will prove that the Yogi teachings are right. This is not the place to discuss the subject fully, but the Yogis know that sex energy may be conserved and used for the development of the body and mind of the individual, instead of being dissipated in unnatural excesses, as is the wont of so many uninformed people. By special request, we'll include here one of the most popular Yogi exercises for this purpose. But whether or not the student wishes to adopt the Yogi theories of continence and clean living, he or she will find that the Complete Breath will do more to restore health to this part of the system than anything else ever tried. Remember, now, we mean normal health, not undue development. The sensualist will find that normal means a lessening of desire, rather than an increase; the weakened man or woman will find a toning up and a relief from the weakness which has heretofore depressed him or her. We do not wish to be misunderstood or misquoted on this subject. The Yogi's ideal is a body strong in all its parts, under the control of a masterful and developed Will, animated by high ideals.

In the practice of the Complete Breath, during inhalation, the diaphragm contracts and exerts a gentle pressure upon the liver, stomach, and other organs, which, in connection with the rhythm of the lungs, acts as a gentle massage of these organs and stimulates their actions, encouraging normal functioning. Each inhalation aids in this internal exercise and assists in causing normal circulation to the organs of nutrition and elimination. In High or Mid Breathing, the organs lose the benefit accrued from this internal massage.

The Western world is paying much attention to Physical Culture just now, which is a good thing. But in their enthusiasm, they must not forget that the exercise of the external muscles is not everything. The internal organs also need exercise, and Nature's plan for this exercise is proper breathing. The diaphragm is Nature's principal instrument for this internal exercise. Its motion vibrates the important organs needed for good nutrition and elimination, and massages and kneads them at each inhalation and exhalation, forcing blood into them and then squeezing it out, and generally toning the organs. Any organ or part of the body which is not exercised gradually atrophies and refuses to function properly, and lack of the internal exercise afforded by the diaphragmatic action leads to diseased organs. The Complete Breath gives the proper motion to the diaphragm, as well as exercising the middle and upper chest. It is indeed "complete" in its actions.

From the standpoint of Western physiology alone, without reference to the Oriental philosophies and sciences, this Yogic system of Complete Breathing is of vital importance to every man, woman, and child who wishes to acquire good health and keep it. Its very simplicity keeps thousands from seriously considering it, while they spend fortunes in seeking optimal health through complicated and expensive "systems." Health knocks at their door, and they don't answer. Verily, the stone which the builders reject is the real cornerstone of the Temple of Health.

—Ramacharaka, Yogi (William Walker Atkinson)
The Hindu-Yogi Science of Breath.

APPENDIX 3: PROGRESS

Progress

DATE: _____

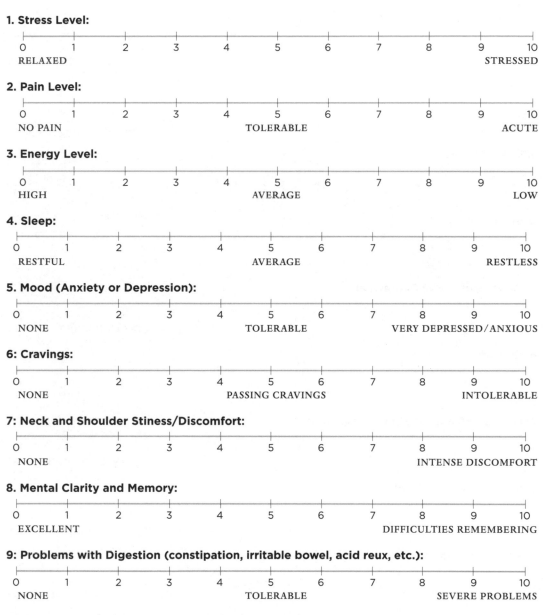

1. Stress Level:

0　1　2　3　4　5　6　7　8　9　10
RELAXED　　　　　　　　　　　　　　　　STRESSED

2. Pain Level:

0　1　2　3　4　5　6　7　8　9　10
NO PAIN　　　　　TOLERABLE　　　　　　ACUTE

3. Energy Level:

0　1　2　3　4　5　6　7　8　9　10
HIGH　　　　　　　AVERAGE　　　　　　　LOW

4. Sleep:

0　1　2　3　4　5　6　7　8　9　10
RESTFUL　　　　　AVERAGE　　　　　　RESTLESS

5. Mood (Anxiety or Depression):

0　1　2　3　4　5　6　7　8　9　10
NONE　　　　　　TOLERABLE　　VERY DEPRESSED/ANXIOUS

6: Cravings:

0　1　2　3　4　5　6　7　8　9　10
NONE　　　　PASSING CRAVINGS　　　INTOLERABLE

7: Neck and Shoulder Stiness/Discomfort:

0　1　2　3　4　5　6　7　8　9　10
NONE　　　　　　　　　　　　　INTENSE DISCOMFORT

8. Mental Clarity and Memory:

0　1　2　3　4　5　6　7　8　9　10
EXCELLENT　　　　　　　　DIFFICULTIES REMEMBERING

9: Problems with Digestion (constipation, irritable bowel, acid reux, etc.):

0　1　2　3　4　5　6　7　8　9　10
NONE　　　　　　TOLERABLE　　　SEVERE PROBLEMS

10: Endurance (self-determined measure):

Progress

DATE: _____

1. Stress Level:

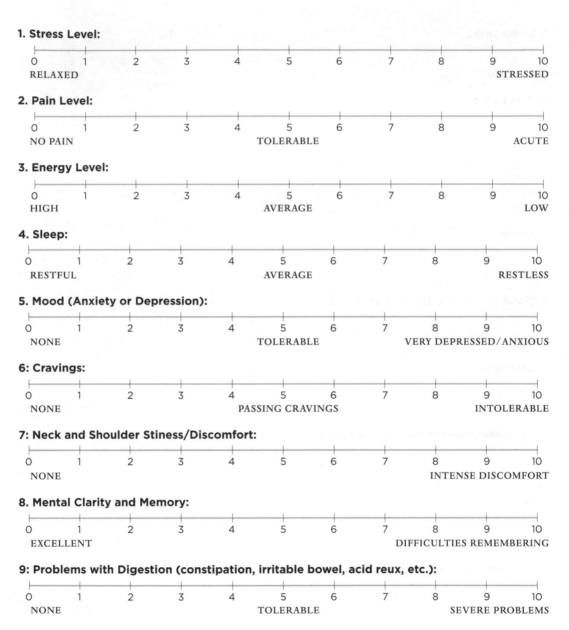

```
0     1     2     3     4     5     6     7     8     9     10
RELAXED                                                STRESSED
```

2. Pain Level:

```
0     1     2     3     4     5     6     7     8     9     10
NO PAIN                  TOLERABLE                        ACUTE
```

3. Energy Level:

```
0     1     2     3     4     5     6     7     8     9     10
HIGH                     AVERAGE                            LOW
```

4. Sleep:

```
0     1     2     3     4     5     6     7     8     9     10
RESTFUL                  AVERAGE                       RESTLESS
```

5. Mood (Anxiety or Depression):

```
0     1     2     3     4     5     6     7     8     9     10
NONE                     TOLERABLE        VERY DEPRESSED/ANXIOUS
```

6: Cravings:

```
0     1     2     3     4     5     6     7     8     9     10
NONE              PASSING CRAVINGS             INTOLERABLE
```

7: Neck and Shoulder Stiness/Discomfort:

```
0     1     2     3     4     5     6     7     8     9     10
NONE                                       INTENSE DISCOMFORT
```

8. Mental Clarity and Memory:

```
0     1     2     3     4     5     6     7     8     9     10
EXCELLENT                         DIFFICULTIES REMEMBERING
```

9: Problems with Digestion (constipation, irritable bowel, acid reux, etc.):

```
0     1     2     3     4     5     6     7     8     9     10
NONE                     TOLERABLE              SEVERE PROBLEMS
```

10: Endurance (self-determined measure):

Progress

DATE: _____

1. Stress Level:

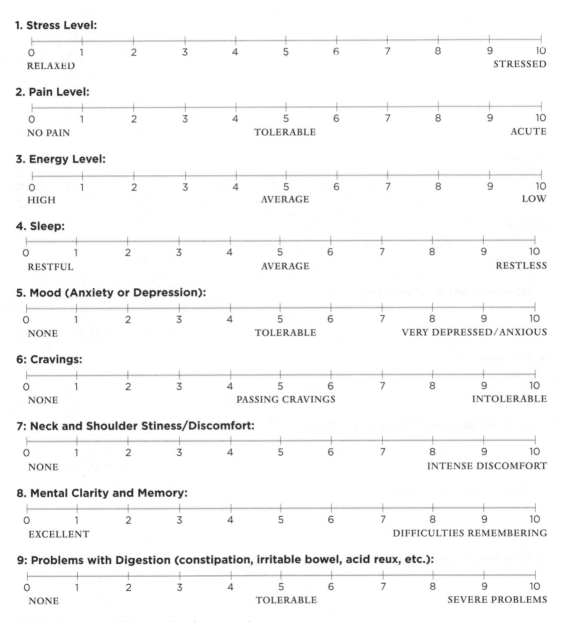

0   1   2   3   4   5   6   7   8   9   10

RELAXED   STRESSED

2. Pain Level:

0   1   2   3   4   5   6   7   8   9   10

NO PAIN   TOLERABLE   ACUTE

3. Energy Level:

0   1   2   3   4   5   6   7   8   9   10

HIGH   AVERAGE   LOW

4. Sleep:

0   1   2   3   4   5   6   7   8   9   10

RESTFUL   AVERAGE   RESTLESS

5. Mood (Anxiety or Depression):

0   1   2   3   4   5   6   7   8   9   10

NONE   TOLERABLE   VERY DEPRESSED/ANXIOUS

6: Cravings:

0   1   2   3   4   5   6   7   8   9   10

NONE   PASSING CRAVINGS   INTOLERABLE

7: Neck and Shoulder Stiness/Discomfort:

0   1   2   3   4   5   6   7   8   9   10

NONE   INTENSE DISCOMFORT

8. Mental Clarity and Memory:

0   1   2   3   4   5   6   7   8   9   10

EXCELLENT   DIFFICULTIES REMEMBERING

9: Problems with Digestion (constipation, irritable bowel, acid reux, etc.):

0   1   2   3   4   5   6   7   8   9   10

NONE   TOLERABLE   SEVERE PROBLEMS

10: Endurance (self-determined measure):

Progress

DATE: _____

1. Stress Level:

| 0 | 1 | 2 | 3 | 4 | 5 | 6 | 7 | 8 | 9 | 10 |
| RELAXED | | | | | | | | | | STRESSED |

2. Pain Level:

| 0 | 1 | 2 | 3 | 4 | 5 | 6 | 7 | 8 | 9 | 10 |
| NO PAIN | | | | | TOLERABLE | | | | | ACUTE |

3. Energy Level:

| 0 | 1 | 2 | 3 | 4 | 5 | 6 | 7 | 8 | 9 | 10 |
| HIGH | | | | | AVERAGE | | | | | LOW |

4. Sleep:

| 0 | 1 | 2 | 3 | 4 | 5 | 6 | 7 | 8 | 9 | 10 |
| RESTFUL | | | | | AVERAGE | | | | | RESTLESS |

5. Mood (Anxiety or Depression):

| 0 | 1 | 2 | 3 | 4 | 5 | 6 | 7 | 8 | 9 | 10 |
| NONE | | | | | TOLERABLE | | | | VERY DEPRESSED/ANXIOUS | |

6: Cravings:

| 0 | 1 | 2 | 3 | 4 | 5 | 6 | 7 | 8 | 9 | 10 |
| NONE | | | | | PASSING CRAVINGS | | | | INTOLERABLE | |

7: Neck and Shoulder Stiness/Discomfort:

| 0 | 1 | 2 | 3 | 4 | 5 | 6 | 7 | 8 | 9 | 10 |
| NONE | | | | | | | | INTENSE DISCOMFORT | | |

8. Mental Clarity and Memory:

| 0 | 1 | 2 | 3 | 4 | 5 | 6 | 7 | 8 | 9 | 10 |
| EXCELLENT | | | | | | | | DIFFICULTIES REMEMBERING | | |

9: Problems with Digestion (constipation, irritable bowel, acid reux, etc.):

| 0 | 1 | 2 | 3 | 4 | 5 | 6 | 7 | 8 | 9 | 10 |
| NONE | | | | | TOLERABLE | | | | SEVERE PROBLEMS | |

10: Endurance (self-determined measure):

Progress

DATE: _____

1. Stress Level:

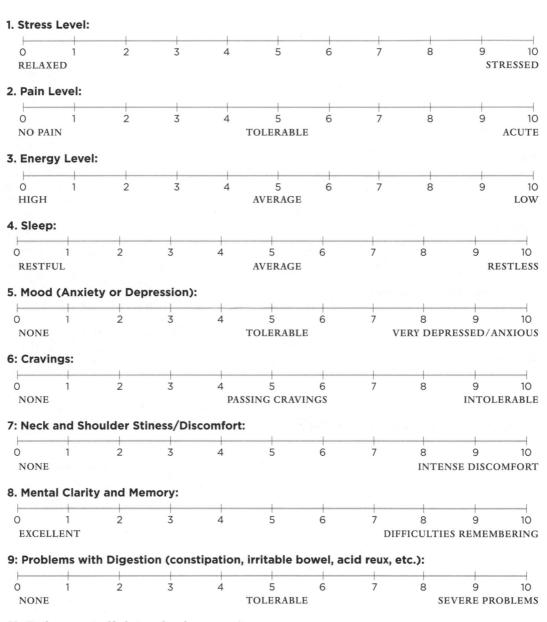

```
0      1      2      3      4      5      6      7      8      9      10
RELAXED                                                        STRESSED
```

2. Pain Level:

```
0      1      2      3      4      5      6      7      8      9      10
NO PAIN                    TOLERABLE                              ACUTE
```

3. Energy Level:

```
0      1      2      3      4      5      6      7      8      9      10
HIGH                       AVERAGE                                 LOW
```

4. Sleep:

```
0      1      2      3      4      5      6      7      8      9      10
RESTFUL                    AVERAGE                            RESTLESS
```

5. Mood (Anxiety or Depression):

```
0      1      2      3      4      5      6      7      8      9      10
NONE                       TOLERABLE            VERY DEPRESSED/ANXIOUS
```

6: Cravings:

```
0      1      2      3      4      5      6      7      8      9      10
NONE                   PASSING CRAVINGS                    INTOLERABLE
```

7: Neck and Shoulder Stiness/Discomfort:

```
0      1      2      3      4      5      6      7      8      9      10
NONE                                                  INTENSE DISCOMFORT
```

8. Mental Clarity and Memory:

```
0      1      2      3      4      5      6      7      8      9      10
EXCELLENT                                      DIFFICULTIES REMEMBERING
```

9: Problems with Digestion (constipation, irritable bowel, acid reux, etc.):

```
0      1      2      3      4      5      6      7      8      9      10
NONE                       TOLERABLE                   SEVERE PROBLEMS
```

10: Endurance (self-determined measure):

Progress

DATE: _____

1. Stress Level:

```
0       1       2       3       4       5       6       7       8       9       10
RELAXED                                                                    STRESSED
```

2. Pain Level:

```
0       1       2       3       4       5       6       7       8       9       10
NO PAIN                         TOLERABLE                                      ACUTE
```

3. Energy Level:

```
0       1       2       3       4       5       6       7       8       9       10
HIGH                            AVERAGE                                          LOW
```

4. Sleep:

```
0       1       2       3       4       5       6       7       8       9       10
RESTFUL                         AVERAGE                                     RESTLESS
```

5. Mood (Anxiety or Depression):

```
0       1       2       3       4       5       6       7       8       9       10
NONE                            TOLERABLE              VERY DEPRESSED/ANXIOUS
```

6: Cravings:

```
0       1       2       3       4       5       6       7       8       9       10
NONE                       PASSING CRAVINGS                          INTOLERABLE
```

7: Neck and Shoulder Stiness/Discomfort:

```
0       1       2       3       4       5       6       7       8       9       10
NONE                                                         INTENSE DISCOMFORT
```

8. Mental Clarity and Memory:

```
0       1       2       3       4       5       6       7       8       9       10
EXCELLENT                                            DIFFICULTIES REMEMBERING
```

9: Problems with Digestion (constipation, irritable bowel, acid reux, etc.):

```
0       1       2       3       4       5       6       7       8       9       10
NONE                            TOLERABLE                      SEVERE PROBLEMS
```

10: Endurance (self-determined measure):

Progress

DATE: _____

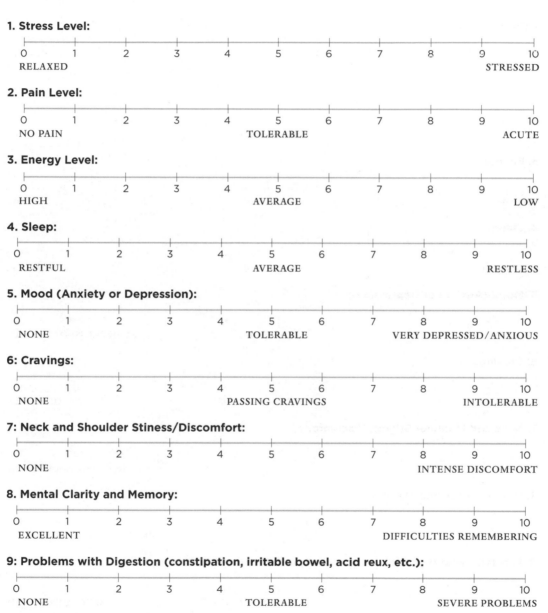

1. Stress Level:

| 0 | 1 | 2 | 3 | 4 | 5 | 6 | 7 | 8 | 9 | 10 |
RELAXED   STRESSED

2. Pain Level:

| 0 | 1 | 2 | 3 | 4 | 5 | 6 | 7 | 8 | 9 | 10 |
NO PAIN   TOLERABLE   ACUTE

3. Energy Level:

| 0 | 1 | 2 | 3 | 4 | 5 | 6 | 7 | 8 | 9 | 10 |
HIGH   AVERAGE   LOW

4. Sleep:

| 0 | 1 | 2 | 3 | 4 | 5 | 6 | 7 | 8 | 9 | 10 |
RESTFUL   AVERAGE   RESTLESS

5. Mood (Anxiety or Depression):

| 0 | 1 | 2 | 3 | 4 | 5 | 6 | 7 | 8 | 9 | 10 |
NONE   TOLERABLE   VERY DEPRESSED/ANXIOUS

6: Cravings:

| 0 | 1 | 2 | 3 | 4 | 5 | 6 | 7 | 8 | 9 | 10 |
NONE   PASSING CRAVINGS   INTOLERABLE

7: Neck and Shoulder Stiness/Discomfort:

| 0 | 1 | 2 | 3 | 4 | 5 | 6 | 7 | 8 | 9 | 10 |
NONE   INTENSE DISCOMFORT

8. Mental Clarity and Memory:

| 0 | 1 | 2 | 3 | 4 | 5 | 6 | 7 | 8 | 9 | 10 |
EXCELLENT   DIFFICULTIES REMEMBERING

9: Problems with Digestion (constipation, irritable bowel, acid reux, etc.):

| 0 | 1 | 2 | 3 | 4 | 5 | 6 | 7 | 8 | 9 | 10 |
NONE   TOLERABLE   SEVERE PROBLEMS

10: Endurance (self-determined measure):

Progress

DATE: _____

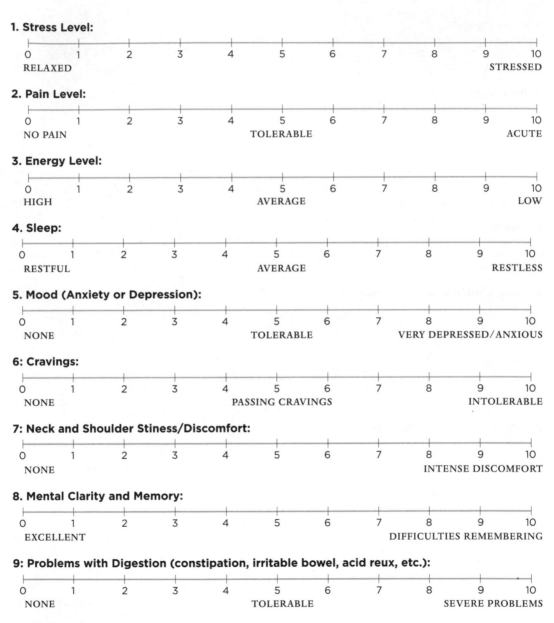

1. Stress Level:

0 1 2 3 4 5 6 7 8 9 10
RELAXED   STRESSED

2. Pain Level:

0 1 2 3 4 5 6 7 8 9 10
NO PAIN   TOLERABLE   ACUTE

3. Energy Level:

0 1 2 3 4 5 6 7 8 9 10
HIGH   AVERAGE   LOW

4. Sleep:

0 1 2 3 4 5 6 7 8 9 10
RESTFUL   AVERAGE   RESTLESS

5. Mood (Anxiety or Depression):

0 1 2 3 4 5 6 7 8 9 10
NONE   TOLERABLE   VERY DEPRESSED/ANXIOUS

6: Cravings:

0 1 2 3 4 5 6 7 8 9 10
NONE   PASSING CRAVINGS   INTOLERABLE

7: Neck and Shoulder Stiness/Discomfort:

0 1 2 3 4 5 6 7 8 9 10
NONE   INTENSE DISCOMFORT

8. Mental Clarity and Memory:

0 1 2 3 4 5 6 7 8 9 10
EXCELLENT   DIFFICULTIES REMEMBERING

9: Problems with Digestion (constipation, irritable bowel, acid reux, etc.):

0 1 2 3 4 5 6 7 8 9 10
NONE   TOLERABLE   SEVERE PROBLEMS

10: Endurance (self-determined measure):

Progress

DATE: _____

1. Stress Level:

```
0       1       2       3       4       5       6       7       8       9       10
RELAXED                                                                    STRESSED
```

2. Pain Level:

```
0       1       2       3       4       5       6       7       8       9       10
NO PAIN                              TOLERABLE                                 ACUTE
```

3. Energy Level:

```
0       1       2       3       4       5       6       7       8       9       10
HIGH                                 AVERAGE                                     LOW
```

4. Sleep:

```
0       1       2       3       4       5       6       7       8       9       10
RESTFUL                              AVERAGE                               RESTLESS
```

5. Mood (Anxiety or Depression):

```
0       1       2       3       4       5       6       7       8       9       10
NONE                                 TOLERABLE           VERY DEPRESSED/ANXIOUS
```

6: Cravings:

```
0       1       2       3       4       5       6       7       8       9       10
NONE                          PASSING CRAVINGS                        INTOLERABLE
```

7: Neck and Shoulder Stiness/Discomfort:

```
0       1       2       3       4       5       6       7       8       9       10
NONE                                                        INTENSE DISCOMFORT
```

8. Mental Clarity and Memory:

```
0       1       2       3       4       5       6       7       8       9       10
EXCELLENT                                               DIFFICULTIES REMEMBERING
```

9: Problems with Digestion (constipation, irritable bowel, acid reux, etc.):

```
0       1       2       3       4       5       6       7       8       9       10
NONE                                 TOLERABLE               SEVERE PROBLEMS
```

10: Endurance (self-determined measure):

Progress

DATE: _____

1. Stress Level:

0	1	2	3	4	5	6	7	8	9	10
RELAXED										STRESSED

2. Pain Level:

0	1	2	3	4	5	6	7	8	9	10
NO PAIN					TOLERABLE					ACUTE

3. Energy Level:

0	1	2	3	4	5	6	7	8	9	10
HIGH					AVERAGE					LOW

4. Sleep:

0	1	2	3	4	5	6	7	8	9	10
RESTFUL					AVERAGE					RESTLESS

5. Mood (Anxiety or Depression):

0	1	2	3	4	5	6	7	8	9	10
NONE					TOLERABLE			VERY DEPRESSED/ANXIOUS		

6: Cravings:

0	1	2	3	4	5	6	7	8	9	10
NONE				PASSING CRAVINGS				INTOLERABLE		

7: Neck and Shoulder Stiness/Discomfort:

0	1	2	3	4	5	6	7	8	9	10
NONE								INTENSE DISCOMFORT		

8. Mental Clarity and Memory:

0	1	2	3	4	5	6	7	8	9	10
EXCELLENT								DIFFICULTIES REMEMBERING		

9: Problems with Digestion (constipation, irritable bowel, acid reux, etc.):

0	1	2	3	4	5	6	7	8	9	10
NONE					TOLERABLE			SEVERE PROBLEMS		

10: Endurance (self-determined measure):

Progress

DATE: _____

1. Stress Level:

```
0     1     2     3     4     5     6     7     8     9     10
RELAXED                                              STRESSED
```

2. Pain Level:

```
0     1     2     3     4     5     6     7     8     9     10
NO PAIN                  TOLERABLE                      ACUTE
```

3. Energy Level:

```
0     1     2     3     4     5     6     7     8     9     10
HIGH                     AVERAGE                          LOW
```

4. Sleep:

```
0     1     2     3     4     5     6     7     8     9     10
RESTFUL                  AVERAGE                     RESTLESS
```

5. Mood (Anxiety or Depression):

```
0     1     2     3     4     5     6     7     8     9     10
NONE                     TOLERABLE       VERY DEPRESSED/ANXIOUS
```

6: Cravings:

```
0     1     2     3     4     5     6     7     8     9     10
NONE              PASSING CRAVINGS            INTOLERABLE
```

7: Neck and Shoulder Stiness/Discomfort:

```
0     1     2     3     4     5     6     7     8     9     10
NONE                                    INTENSE DISCOMFORT
```

8. Mental Clarity and Memory:

```
0     1     2     3     4     5     6     7     8     9     10
EXCELLENT                          DIFFICULTIES REMEMBERING
```

9: Problems with Digestion (constipation, irritable bowel, acid reux, etc.):

```
0     1     2     3     4     5     6     7     8     9     10
NONE                     TOLERABLE          SEVERE PROBLEMS
```

10: Endurance (self-determined measure):

Progress

DATE: _____

1. Stress Level:

```
  0     1     2     3     4     5     6     7     8     9     10
RELAXED                                                    STRESSED
```

2. Pain Level:

```
  0     1     2     3     4     5     6     7     8     9     10
NO PAIN                   TOLERABLE                          ACUTE
```

3. Energy Level:

```
  0     1     2     3     4     5     6     7     8     9     10
 HIGH                      AVERAGE                            LOW
```

4. Sleep:

```
  0     1     2     3     4     5     6     7     8     9     10
RESTFUL                    AVERAGE                         RESTLESS
```

5. Mood (Anxiety or Depression):

```
  0     1     2     3     4     5     6     7     8     9     10
 NONE                     TOLERABLE        VERY DEPRESSED/ANXIOUS
```

6: Cravings:

```
  0     1     2     3     4     5     6     7     8     9     10
 NONE               PASSING CRAVINGS              INTOLERABLE
```

7: Neck and Shoulder Stiness/Discomfort:

```
  0     1     2     3     4     5     6     7     8     9     10
 NONE                                       INTENSE DISCOMFORT
```

8. Mental Clarity and Memory:

```
  0     1     2     3     4     5     6     7     8     9     10
EXCELLENT                               DIFFICULTIES REMEMBERING
```

9: Problems with Digestion (constipation, irritable bowel, acid reux, etc.):

```
  0     1     2     3     4     5     6     7     8     9     10
 NONE                     TOLERABLE            SEVERE PROBLEMS
```

10: Endurance (self-determined measure):

Progress

DATE: _____

1. Stress Level:

```
0     1     2     3     4     5     6     7     8     9     10
RELAXED                                                STRESSED
```

2. Pain Level:

```
0     1     2     3     4     5     6     7     8     9     10
NO PAIN                  TOLERABLE                        ACUTE
```

3. Energy Level:

```
0     1     2     3     4     5     6     7     8     9     10
HIGH                     AVERAGE                            LOW
```

4. Sleep:

```
0     1     2     3     4     5     6     7     8     9     10
RESTFUL                  AVERAGE                       RESTLESS
```

5. Mood (Anxiety or Depression):

```
0     1     2     3     4     5     6     7     8     9     10
NONE                     TOLERABLE          VERY DEPRESSED/ANXIOUS
```

6: Cravings:

```
0     1     2     3     4     5     6     7     8     9     10
NONE                 PASSING CRAVINGS           INTOLERABLE
```

7: Neck and Shoulder Stiness/Discomfort:

```
0     1     2     3     4     5     6     7     8     9     10
NONE                                          INTENSE DISCOMFORT
```

8. Mental Clarity and Memory:

```
0     1     2     3     4     5     6     7     8     9     10
EXCELLENT                            DIFFICULTIES REMEMBERING
```

9: Problems with Digestion (constipation, irritable bowel, acid reux, etc.):

```
0     1     2     3     4     5     6     7     8     9     10
NONE                     TOLERABLE          SEVERE PROBLEMS
```

10: Endurance (self-determined measure):

Progress

DATE: _____

1. Stress Level:

```
0     1     2     3     4     5     6     7     8     9     10
RELAXED                                              STRESSED
```

2. Pain Level:

```
0     1     2     3     4     5     6     7     8     9     10
NO PAIN              TOLERABLE                         ACUTE
```

3. Energy Level:

```
0     1     2     3     4     5     6     7     8     9     10
HIGH                 AVERAGE                            LOW
```

4. Sleep:

```
0     1     2     3     4     5     6     7     8     9     10
RESTFUL              AVERAGE                         RESTLESS
```

5. Mood (Anxiety or Depression):

```
0     1     2     3     4     5     6     7     8     9     10
NONE                 TOLERABLE           VERY DEPRESSED/ANXIOUS
```

6: Cravings:

```
0     1     2     3     4     5     6     7     8     9     10
NONE              PASSING CRAVINGS              INTOLERABLE
```

7: Neck and Shoulder Stiness/Discomfort:

```
0     1     2     3     4     5     6     7     8     9     10
NONE                                    INTENSE DISCOMFORT
```

8. Mental Clarity and Memory:

```
0     1     2     3     4     5     6     7     8     9     10
EXCELLENT                           DIFFICULTIES REMEMBERING
```

9: Problems with Digestion (constipation, irritable bowel, acid reux, etc.):

```
0     1     2     3     4     5     6     7     8     9     10
NONE                 TOLERABLE              SEVERE PROBLEMS
```

10: Endurance (self-determined measure):

BIBLIOGRAPHY AND RECOMMENDED READING

Acharya, U. Rajendra, K. Paul Joseph, N. Kannathal, Lim Choo Min, and Jasjit S. Suri. "Heart Rate Variability." In *Advances in Cardiac Signal Processing*, edited by U. Rajendra Acharya, Jasjit S. Suri, Jos A. E. Spaan, and Shankar M. Krishnan, 121–65. Berlin-Heidelberg: Springer-Verlag, 2007.

Altman, Nathaniel. *The Oxygen Prescription: The Miracle of Oxidative Therapies*. Rochester, Vermont: Healing Arts, 2007.

Ancell, Henry. *A Treatise on Tuberculosis: The Constitutional Origin of Consumption and Scrofula*. London: Longman, Brown, Green and Longmans, 1852.

Anderson, Bert, and Ronald Ley. "Dyspnea during Panic Attacks: An Internet Survey of Incidences of Changes in Breathing." *Behavior Modification* 25, no. 4 (2001): 546–54.

Anderson, D. E., J. D. McNeely, and B. G. Windham. "Regular Slow-breathing Exercise Effects on Blood Pressure and Breathing Patterns at Rest." *Journal of Human Hypertension* 24, no. 12 (2010): 807–13.

Avidan, B., A. Sonnenberg, T. G. Schnell, and S. J. Sontag. "Walking and Chewing Reduce Postprandial Acid Reflux." *Alimentary Pharmacology & Therapeutics* 15, no. 2 (2001): 151–55.

Beard, James. *Thirteen Breaths to Freedom: An Introduction to Breathwork*. San Diego: Sacred Systems, 2011.

Beauchaine, Theodore. "Vagal Tone, Development, and Gray's Motivational Theory: Toward an Integrated Model of Autonomic Nervous System Functioning in Psychopathology." *Development and Psychopathology* 13, no. 2 (2001): 183–214.

Bergmark, Anders. "Stability of the Lumbar Spine: A Study in Mechanical Engineering." *Acta Orthopaedica Scandinavica* 60, no. 230 (1989): 1–54.

Bilchick, Kenneth C., and Ronald D. Berger. "Heart Rate Variability." *Journal of Cardiovascular Electrophysiology* 17, no. 6 (2006): 691–94.

Bohns, Vanessa K., and Scott S. Wiltermuth. "It Hurts When I Do This (or You Do That): Posture and Pain Tolerance." *Journal of Experimental Social Psychology* 48, no. 1 (2012): 341–45.

Borrow, Sharon J., British Snoring and Sleep Apnoea Association. "The Stages of Snoring." Accessed May 25, 2016. http://www.britishsnoring .co.uk/stages_of_snoring.php.

Boyle, Kyndall L., Josh Olinick, and Cynthia Lewis. "Clinical Suggestion: The Value of Blowing Up a Balloon." *North American Journal of Sports Physical Therapy* 5, no. 3 (2010): 179–88.

Boyle, Mike. "The Joint-by-Joint Concept (Appendix 1)." In *Movement: Functional Movement Systems* by Gray Cook, 319–21. Aptos, California: On-Target Publications, 2012.

Brown, Richard P., and Patricia L. Gerbarg. "*Sudarshan Kriya* Yogic Breathing in the Treatment of Stress, Anxiety, and Depression: Part I—Neurophysiologic Model." *Journal of Alternative & Complementary Medicine* 11, no. 1 (2005): 189–201.

———*The Healing Power of the Breath: Simple Techniques to Reduce Stress and Anxiety, Enhance Concentration, and Balance Your Emotions.* Boulder, Colorado: Shambhala Publications, 2012.

Butler, James P., Stephen H. Loring, Samuel Patz, Akira Tsuda, Dmitriy A. Yablonskiy, and Steven J. Mentzer. "Evidence for Adult Lung Growth in Humans." *New England Journal of Medicine* 367 (2012): 244–47.

Cailliet, Rene, and Leonard Gross. *The Rejuvenation Strategy: A Medically Approved Fitness Program to Reverse the Effects of Aging.* New York: Doubleday, 1987.

Calabrese, Lauren. "Volume of Human Lungs," The Physics Factbook, accessed May 25, 2016, http://hypertextbook.com/facts/2001 /LaurenCalabrese.shtml.

Calais-Germain, Blandine. *Anatomy of Breathing.* Vista, California: Eastland Press, 2006.

Chiang, Li-Chi, Wei-Fen Ma, Jing-Long Huang, Li-Feng Tseng, and Kai-Chung Hsueh. "Effect of Relaxation-breathing Training on Anxiety and Asthma Signs/Symptoms of Children with Moderate-to-severe Asthma: A Randomized Controlled Trial." *International Journal of Nursing Studies* 46, no. 8 (2009): 1061–70.

Coates, Budd, and Claire Kowalchik. *Runner's World Running on Air: The Revolutionary Way to Run Better by Breathing Smarter.* Emmaus, Pennsylvania: Rodale Books, 2013.

Conrad, Ansgar, Anett Müller, Sigrun Doberenz, Sunyoung Kim, Alicia E. Meuret, Eileen Wollburg, and Walton T. Roth. "Psychophysiological Effects of Breathing Instructions for Stress Management." *Applied Psychophysiological Biofeedback* 32, no. 2 (2007): 89–98.

Cook, Gray. *Movement: Functional Movement Systems.* Aptos, California: On-Target Publications, 2012.

Cuddy, Amy. *Presence: Bringing Your Boldest Self to Your Biggest Challenges.* New York: Little, Brown and Company, 2015.

Davies, Gwyneth A., and Charlotte E. Bolton. "Age-related Changes in the Respiratory System." In *Brocklehurst's Textbook of Geriatric Medicine and Gerontology.* Philadelphia: Elsevier Saunders, 2010.

DeSimone, M. Elayne, and Amanda Crowe. "Nonpharmacological Approaches in the Management of Hypertension." *Journal of the American Academy of Nurse Practitioners* 21, no. 4 (2009): 189–96.

Divine, Mark. *Unbeatable Mind.* Scotts Valley, California: Create Space, 2014.

Doidge, Norman. *The Brain That Changes Itself: Stories of Personal Triumph from the Frontiers of Brain Science.* New York: Penguin, 2007.

Elliott, David. *Healing.* Los Angeles: Hawk Press, 2010.

Engles, Lisa. *Breathe Run Breathe.* Seattle: Amazon, 2013. Kindle e-book.

Farhi, Donna. *The Breathing Book: Good Health and Vitality through Essential Breath Work.* New York: Holt Paperbacks, 1996.

Fitzpatrick, M. F., H. McLean, A. M. Urton, A. Tan, D. O'Donnell, and H. S. Driver. "Effect of Nasal or Oral Breathing Route on Upper Airway Resistance During Sleep." *European Respiratory Journal* 22, no. 5 (2003): 827–32.

Gallego, Jorge, Elise Nsegbe, and Estelle Durand. "Learning in Respiratory Control." *Behavior Modification* 25, no. 4 (2001): 495–512.

Garfinkel, Marian S., Atul Singhal, Warren A. Katz, David A. Allan,

Rosemary Reshetar, and H. Ralph Schumacher. "Yoga-based Intervention for Carpal Tunnel Syndrome: A Randomized Trial." *Journal of the American Medical Association* 280, no. 18 (1998): 1601–03.

George, Robert "Skip." "Breathe Well and Breathe Often: Defining and Correcting Dysfunctional Breathing Patterns." *Dynamic Chiropractic* 31, no. 22 (2012): 112–21.

Gladwell, Malcolm. *David and Goliath: Underdogs, Misfits, and the Art of Battling Giants*. New York: Back Bay Books, 2015.

Goldstein, David S., David Robertson, Murray Esler, Stephen E. Straus, and Graeme Eisenhofer. "Dysautonomias: Clinical Disorders of the Autonomic Nervous System." *Annals of Internal Medicine* 137, no. 9 (2002): 753–63.

Grof, Stanislav, Christina Grof, and Jack Kornfield. *Holotropic Breathwork*. Albany: State University of New York Press, 2010.

Grossman, Dave. *On Combat: The Psychology and Physiology of Deadly Conflict in War and in Peace*. Millstadt, Illinois: Human Factor Research Group, 2012.

Grout, Pam. *Jumpstart Your Metabolism: How to Lose Weight by Changing the Way You Breathe*. New York: Simon & Schuster, 1998.

Hall, John E. *Guyton and Hall Textbook of Medical Physiology*, 13th ed. Philadelphia: W. B. Saunders, 2015.

Hanh, Thich Nhat. *Breathe! You Are Alive: Sutra on the Full Awareness of Breathing*. London: Rider, 1992.

Hargreave, F. E., and K. Parameswaran. "Asthma, COPD and Bronchitis Are Just Components of Airway Disease." *European Respiratory Journal* 28, no. 2 (2006): 264–67.

Harms, Craig A., Thomas J. Wetter, Claudette M. St. Croix, David F. Pegelow, and Jerome A. Dempsey. "Effects of Respiratory Muscle Work on Exercise Performance." *Journal of Applied Physiology* 89, no. 1 (2000): 1131–38.

Hatherley, Paul. *The Internal Development Necessary to Become Loving and Wise*. Bloomington: Balboa Press, 2011.

Hendler, Sheldon Saul. *The Oxygen Breakthrough: 30 Days to an Illness-free Life*. New York: William Morrow, 1989.

Hendricks, Gay. *Conscious Breathing: Breathwork for Health, Stress Release, and Personal Mastery*. New York: Bantam, 2010.

Huffington, Arianna. *The Sleep Revolution: Transforming Your Life, One Night at a Time*. New York: Harmony, 2016.

Hülsheger, Ute R., Hugo J. E. M. Alberts, Alina Feinholdt, and Jonas W. B. Lang. "Benefits of Mindfulness at Work: The Role of Mindfulness in Emotion Regulation, Emotional Exhaustion, and Job Satisfaction." *Journal of Applied Psychology* 98, no. 2 (2013): 310–25.

Iyengar, B. K. S. *Light on Prānāyāma: The Yogic Art of Breathing*. New York: Crossroad Publishing, 1985.

Jones, B., and Gray Cook. "Functional Movement System." *North American Journal of Sports Physical Therapy* 1, no. 3 (2006): 28–35.

Kapandji, I. A. *Physiology of the Joints*, vol. 3. London: Churchill Livingstone, 2008.

Kaushi, Rajeev Mohan, Reshma Kaushik, Sukhdev Krishan Mahajan, and Vemreddi Rajesh. "Effects of Mental Relaxation and Slow Breathing in Essential Hypertension." *Complementary Therapies in Medicine* 14, no. 2 (2006): 120–26.

Khalsa, Gurucharan, and Yogi Bhajan. *Breathwalk: Breathing Your Way to a Revitalized Body, Mind, and Spirit*. New York: Broadway Books, 2000.

Kim, Sang H. *Power Breathing: Breathe Your Way to Inner Power, Stress Reduction, Performance Enhancement, Optimum Health and Fitness*. Cape Cod: Turtle Press, 2008.

Kornfield, Jack, and Daniel J. Siegel. *Mindfulness and the Brain: A Professional Training in the Science and Practice of Meditative Awareness*. Louisville, Colorado: Sounds True, 2010.

Kravitz, Judith. *Breathe Deep Laugh Loudly: The Joy of Transformational Breathing*. New York: Free Press, 1999.

Kryger, Meir H., Thomas Roth, and William C. Dement. *Principles and Practice of Sleep Medicine*. Philadelphia: W. B. Saunders, 2005.

Kubin, Leszek, George F. Alheid, Edward J. Zuperku, and Donald R. McCrimmon. "Central Pathways of Pulmonary and Lower Airway Vagal Afferents." *Journal of Applied Physiology* 101, no. 2 (2006): 610–56.

La Rovere, M. T. "Heart Rate Variability." *Giornale Italiano di Aritmologia* 10, no. 1 (2007): 20–23.

Larzelere, Michele M., and Glenn N. Jones. "Stress and Health." *Primary Care: Clinics in Office Practice* 35, no. 4 (2008): 839–56.

Lazar, Sara W., Catherine E. Kerr, Rachel H. Wasserman, Jeremy R.

Gray, et al. "Meditation Experience Is Associated with Increased Cortical Thickness." *NeuroReport* 16, no. 17 (2005): 1893–97.

Lee, Al, and Don Campbell. *Perfect Breathing: Transform Your Life One Breath at a Time.* New York: Sterling, 2009.

Lee, Diane G. *The Pelvic Girdle: An Integration of Clinical Expertise and Research.* London: Churchill Livingstone, 2010.

Lehrer, Paul M. "Emotionally Triggered Asthma: A Review of Research Literature and Some Hypotheses for Self-regulation Therapies." *Applied Psychophysiology and Biofeedback* 23, no. 1 (1998): 13–42.

Lewis, Dennis. *Free Your Breath, Free Your Life: How Conscious Breathing Can Relieve Stress, Increase Vitality, and Help You Live More Fully.* Boulder, Colorado: Shambhala, 2004.

Ley, R. "The Modification of Breathing Behavior: Pavlovian and Operant Control in Emotion and Cognition." *Behavior Modification* no. 3 (1999): 441–79.

Liem, Karel F. "Form and Function of Lungs: The Evolution of Air Breathing Mechanisms." *American Zoologist* 28, no. 2 (1998): 730–45.

Loehr, James, and Jeffrey Midgow. *Breathe In, Breathe Out: Inhale Energy and Exhale Stress by Guiding and Controlling Your Breathing.* Fairfax, Virginia: Time-Life Books, 1999.

Martin, D. "Inspiratory Muscle Strength Training Improves Weaning Outcome in Failure to Wean Patients: A Randomized Trial." *Critical Care* no. 2 (2011): 62–78.

McConnell, Alison. *Breathe Strong, Perform Better.* Champaign, Illinois: Human Kinetics, 2011.

McGill, S. M., M. T. Sharratt, and J. P. Sequin. "Loads on the Spinal Tissues During Simultaneous Lifting and Ventilator Challenge." *Ergonomics* 38 (1995): 1772–92.

McIntosh, Daniel N., R. B. Zajonc, Peter S. Vig, and Stephen W. Emerick. "Facial Movement, Breathing, Temperature, and Affect: Implications of the Vascular Theory of Emotional Efference." *Cognition and Emotion* 11, no. 2 (1997): 171–96.

McKeown, Patrick. *The Oxygen Advantage.* William Morrow, 2015.

Meles, E., C. Giannattasio, M. Failla, G. Gentile, A. Capra, and G. Mancia. "Nonpharmacologic Treatment of Hypertension by Respiratory

Exercise in the Home Setting." *American Journal of Hypertension* 17, no. 4 (2004): 370–74.

Moss, M. C., and A. B. Scholey. "Oxygen Administration Enhances Memory Formation in Healthy Young Adults." *Psychopharmacology* 124, no. 3 (1996): 255–60.

O'Connell, Dennis, Janelle O'Connell, and Martha Hinman. *Special Tests of the Cardiovascular, Pulmonary, and Gastrointestinal Systems.* Thorofare, New Jersey: SLACK Publishing, 2010.

Öhman, Arne, Alfons Hamm, and Kenneth Hugdahl. "Cognition and the Autonomic Nervous System: Orienting, Anticipation, and Conditioning." In *Handbook of Psychophysiology*, edited by John T. Cacioppo. New York: Cambridge University Press, 2000.

Okuro, R. T., A. M. Morcillo, M. A. Ribiero, E. Sakano, P. B. Conti, and J. D. Ribiero. "Mouth Breathing and Forward Head Posture." *Jornal Brasileiro de Pneumologia* 37, no. 4 (2011): 471–79.

Osho. *Meditation: The First and Last Freedom.* New York: St. Martin's Griffin, 2004.

Palastanga, Nigel, and Roger Soames. *Anatomy and Human Movement: Structure and Function.* London: Churchill Livingstone, 2012.

Parati, G., and R. Carretta. "Device-guided Slow Breathing as a Non-pharmacological Approach to Antihypertensive Treatment: Efficacy, Problems and Perspectives." *American Journal of Hypertension* 25, no. 1 (2007): 24–59.

Perri, Maria. "Rehabilitation of Breathing Pattern Disorders." In *Rehabilitation of the Spine: A Practitioner's Manual*, edited by Craig Liebenson. Philadelphia: Lippincott Williams & Wilkins, 2007.

Pinna, G. D., R. Maestri, and M. T. La Rovere. "Effect of Paced Breathing on Ventilatory and Cardiovascular Variability Parameters During Short-term Investigations of Autonomic Function." *American Journal of Physiology—Heart and Circulatory Physiology* 290, no. 1 (2006): 400–24.

Ray, Reginald A. *Your Breathing Body.* Sounds True, 2008, compact disc.

Romano, Antonino D., Gaetano Serviddio, Angela de Matthaeis, Francesco Bellanti, and Gianluigi Vendemiale. "Oxidative Stress and Aging." *Journal of Nephrology* 23, no. 15 (2010): 29–36.

Sapolsky, Robert M. *Why Zebras Don't Get Ulcers*. New York: Holt Paperbacks, 2004.

Sarno, John E. *The Mindbody Prescription: Healing the Body, Healing the Pain*. New York: Warner, 1999.

———*Healing Back Pain: The Mind-Body Connection*. New York: Grand Central Life and Style, 2010.

Scholey, Andrew B., Mark C. Moss, and Keith Wesnes. "Oxygen and Cognitive Performance: The Temporal Relationship between Hyperoxia and Enhanced Memory." *Psychopharmacology* 140, no. 1 (1998): 123–26.

Schunemann, Holger J., Joan Dorn, Brydon J. B. Grant, Warren Winkelstein Jr., and Maurizio Trevisan. "Pulmonary Function Is a Long-term Predictor of Mortality in the General Population: 29-Year Follow-up of the Buffalo Health Study." *Chest* 118, no. 3 (2000): 656–64.

Seppälä, Emma M. "20 Scientific Reasons to Start Meditating Today." *Psychology Today*, September 2013.

Severinsen, Stig Avall. *Breatheology: Optimize Your Health and Performance*. Naples: Idelson Gnocchi, 2010.

Seyle, Hans. *Stress without Distress*. Philadelphia: Lippincott Williams & Wilkins, 1974.

Sims, N. R., J. M. Finegan, J. P. Blass, D. M. Bowen, and D. Neary. "Mitochondrial Function in Brain Tissue in Primary Degenerative Dementia." *Brain Research* 436, no. 1 (1987): 30–38.

Smith, J. C., A. P. L. Abdala, H. Koizumi, I. A. Rybak, and J. F. R. Paton. "Spatial and Functional Architecture of the Mammalian Brain Stem Respiratory Network: A Hierarchy of Three Oscillatory Mechanisms." *Journal of Neurophysiology* 98, no. 6 (2007): 370–87.

Smith, Michelle D., Anne Russell, and Paul W. Hodges. "The Relationship between Incontinence, Breathing Disorders, Gastrointestinal Symptoms, and Back Pain in Women: A Longitudinal Cohort Study." *Clinical Journal of Pain* 30, no. 2 (2014): 162–67.

Storm, Max. *A Life Worth Breathing*. New York: Skyhorse Publishing, 2012.

Taylor, Kylea, Leonard Orr, Jim Morningstar, and Sondra Ray. *The Complete Breath: A Professional Guide to Health and Wellbeing*. Milwaukee: Transformations Incorporated, 2012.

Telles, S., and T. Desiraju. "Heart Rate Alterations in Different Types of Pranayamas." *Indian Journal of Physiology and Pharmacology* 36, no. 4 (1993): 287–88.

———"Oxygen Consumption during Pranayamic Type of Very Slow-rate Breathing." *Indian Journal of Medical Research* 94 (1991): 357–63 .

Van Den Wittenboer, Godfried, Kees Van Der Wolf, and Jan Van Dixhoorn. "Respiratory Variability and Psychological Well-being in Schoolchildren." *Behavior Modification* 27, no. 5 (2003): 653–70.

Van Dixhoorn, J., and H. J. Duivenvoorden. "Efficacy of Nijmegen Questionnaire in Recognition of the Hyperventilation Syndrome." *Journal of Psychosomatic Research* 29, no. 2 (1985): 199–206.

Vaughn, Dan. "Looking Forward." *Journal of Manual and Manipulative Therapy* 21, no. 4 (2013): 175–76.

Viskoper, Reuven, Irena Shapira, Rita Priluck, Rina Mindlin, et al. "Non-pharmacologic Treatment of Resistant Hypertensives by Device-guided Slow Breathing Exercises." *American Journal of Hypertension* 16, no. 6 (2003): 484–87.

Weil, Andrew. *Breathing: The Master Key to Self-healing.* Louisville, Colorado: Sounds True, 1999.

West, John B. *Respiratory Physiology: The Essentials.* Philadelphia: Lippincott Williams & Wilkins, 2008.

West, Kathleen E., Michael R. Jablonski, Benjamin Warfield, Kate S. Cecil, et al. "Blue Light from Light-emitting Diodes Elicits a Dose-dependent Suppression of Melatonin in Humans." *Journal of Applied Psychology* 110, no. 3 (2011): 619–26.

Wilhelm, Frank H., Richard Gevirtz, and Walton T. Roth. "Respiratory Dysregulation in Anxiety, Functional Cardiac, and Pain Disorders: Assessment, Phenomenology, and Treatment." *Behavior Modification* 25, no. 4 (2001): 513–45.

Woodyard, Catherine. "Exploring the Therapeutic Effects of Yoga and Its Ability to Increase Quality of Life." *International Journal of Yoga* 4, no. 2 (2011): 49–54.

Yee, Rodney. *Relaxation and Breathing for Meditation.* Gaiam, 2003, DVD.

Yogi Ramacharaka (William Walker Atkinson). *The Hindu-Yogi Science of Breath.* Chicago: Yogi Publication Society, 1905.

INDEX

Page numbers followed by "n" indicate information found in footnotes.

ABOUT THE AUTHOR

Belisa Vranich PsyD is a renowned clinical psychologist, public speaker, and founder of The Breathing Class™. Belisa has taught and lectured across the USA on topics related to dysfunctional breathing patterns and stress. The Breathing Class™ has been reviewed by a wide variety of publications including *O The Oprah Magazine, The Wall Street Journal, Men's Journal, Men's Health and Fitness,* and others. She is a current member of Global Breathwork Practitioners.

Belisa was previously the Health and Sex Editor at *Men's Fitness* magazine USA, a relationship expert for *Men's Health* USA. Belisa has been interviewed as an expert in numerous publications in the USA, including *The Wall Street Journal, Cosmopolitan, Seventeen, Good Housekeeping* and *Parenting,* and has also served as an advisor for *Shape* magazine USA. Belisa is a regular guest on numerous USA television shows including CNN, Fox News, the Today Show and Good Morning America.

Belisa received her doctorate degree in Psychology from New York University. After fifteen years of experience in private practice, she is recognized as a leading expert in topics that range from health and fitness, stress reduction, nutrition, relationships, to trauma and addiction. Previously, she was the Director of Public Education at the Mental Health Association of New York City; she co-taught Personality Assessment and Projective Techniques at New York University; she was a consultant at the National Mental Health Association in Washington; director of an outpatient clinic at Jacobi Hospital Center, New York City; a school psychologist in the South Bronx; and part of the Brooklyn Aids Task Force supporting parolees and their families.

An outspoken advocate for women's health issues and veterans' rights, Belisa also volunteers with several animal rescue organizations in New York City and Los Angeles. She is an advisory board member of Philosophy's Hope and Grace Mental Health Campaign.

www.thebreathingclass.com

HAY HOUSE

Look within

Join the conversation about latest products,
events, exclusive offers and more.

f Hay House UK

🐦 @HayHouseUK

📷 @hayhouseuk

♥ healyourlife.com

We'd love to hear from you!